"Sustainable means: 'still running and alive in ten years from now,' applying the same to businesses, projects, entrepreneurs and also to policies and beings. CSR is instrumental to all of them; it is a no-brainer. This book, with its exclusive true stories of success, shows that sound CSR is not only easy to do, but also leads to business longevity when led by visionaries."

Joaquin Velazquez-Boston

Chairman of International Board of Business Owners, Global Actors & Entrepreneurs for Sustainability (Entreps Global), cum laude researcher on competitiveness, leadership and success, senior international advisor and member of the Board at the United Nations' promoted UNGSII, and vice-president of JEUNE

"The world is being required to wake up to the fundamental truth that we are indeed connected – separation and concepts of 'I,' 'Me' and 'Mine' have got us into this mess. It is time not only to realize but to live the truth: that we are not separate from each other or from our planet. Perhaps then we have a chance to heal the scars of racial division and planetary destruction."

Sahera Chohan

Former BBC TV presenter, author, speaker and leadership coach

"This highly engaging and on point book couldn't have come at a better time. Modern society is in urgent need of change. Through inspiring vision and compelling narrative of the future we want to create, we will find the energy to get there. So many important and powerful voices have been hushed due to fear of greenwash accusations, and so much motivation has been lost due to deceit and disappointment. For business to not only survive but thrive as a valuable contributor to society, CSR must be genuine, and PR, when from a place of truth, can be the wind in the wings. Sangeeta writes from a place of such compassion and professionalism with a deep understanding of the fundamentals and the future for PR and CSR. A must-read for any business owner."

Claire O'Neill
Co-founder and director,
A Greener Festival Ltd

"At Unwrpd, every pound, dollar and euro consumers spend with us is a vote for the world they want to live in. We give consumers the simplest means of pushing for a more sustainable future and we need more businesses like ours to drive this agenda forward; this book puts the how and why into context."

Daniel Hemsley
Founder of Unwrpd

"It doesn't matter what industry we are in; we can all do better. The pandemic has shown us how interconnected we are, where those brands with strong CSR values have been able to lead the way. Consumers want to engage with companies that have purpose – who are investing in the future of their communities and the environment. But it needs to be genuine! This book will help you find your way – how to do business better without the hyperbole."

Yosien Burke
Business and sustainability development in UK film and TV production industry

"During these unprecedented times, it is paramount for all businesses to thoughtfully redefine their core competencies, particularly their CSR commitments. If more corporations adopt meaningful CSR practices, this world will fundamentally become better, less wasteful, more productive – Sangeeta's book helps to articulate the foundation of those principals with shining pre- and post-pandemic examples of who has got it right."

Chef Jainine Jaffer
2020 Silver State Award recipient for Best Female Chef and entrepreneur, Las Vegas

"Good and honest fulfilment of CSR is a necessary condition for good and honest PR. The book elucidates opportunities of leveraging and the perils of confusing the two."

Deepak Arora
one of India's respected voices on CSR and thought leader specializing in public policy/affairs, rural development and enterprise development

Published by
LID Publishing Limited
The Record Hall, Studio 304,
16-16a Baldwins Gardens,
London EC1N 7RJ, UK

info@lidpublishing.com
www.lidpublishing.com

A member of:

BPR
businesspublishersroundtable.com

© Sangeeta Waldron, 2021
© LID Publishing Limited, 2021

Printed by CPI Group (UK) Ltd, Croydon CR0 4YY

ISBN: 978-1-911671-42-8
ISBN: 978-1-911671-43-5 (ebook)

Cover and page design: Caroline Li

Sangeeta Waldron

CORPORATE SOCIAL RESPONSIBILITY IS NOT PUBLIC RELATIONS

How to put CSR at the heart of your company and maximize the business benefits

MADRID | MEXICO CITY | LONDON
NEW YORK | BUENOS AIRES
BOGOTA | SHANGHAI | NEW DELHI

Table of Contents

Acknowledgements

This book has received enormous amounts of goodwill and support along the way, and I would like to thank each of the thought leaders and entrepreneurs who gave their time to be interviewed. Each of these conversations have added to the strength of the book.

I am especially grateful to Lucy Siegle, who is known for creating strong and meaningful conversations about sustainability in businesses and CSR, for writing the foreword. We could all do with more people like Lucy and the work she does in driving awareness of what needs to be done to help our planet and where we have been failing.

I also would like to thank everyone at LID Publishing, especially Martin Liu, for believing in me and this book.

During the time I was writing this book, I lost my mum, which made it difficult to write in the beginning. My head was foggy with grief, but the fog lifted through the love and support of family and friends. I want to thank the extended Waldron family for all their love.

And finally, I dedicate this book to #teamWaldron – Steve, my husband and Rory, our son. Together, they are the dream team in every way possible. You both always enable me to fly high... and, of course, a special thank you to my mum, who has been guiding me throughout.

Foreword

As this book gathered shape and form in a very modern way – I began following the author, Sangeeta, and sharing ideas on social media – she sent me some extracts, followed by an iteration close to the finished version you read now. I was intrigued, and began dipping in. I noticed that I used this book as a confidence booster and when I wanted to bolster my own ideas with some straightforward, clear-sighted explanations of the terms and workings of CSR. So, the first thing I have to say about this book is that you will find it enormously sustaining (a good thing given the subject!).

But I *really* immersed myself in this book one Monday morning, in between Zoom panel debates. In our social media friendship, Zoom-centric working day, the setup might all seem very 'now,' but actually I'd just had a frustrating panel debate that could have happened any time in the last five to ten years. It was one of those industry sustainability panels (I'd been invited to speak about packaging and the circular economy) where there was a slightly frosty tone to the questioning. The request was implicit – could I tone down my asks of a new sustainable paradigm that was in step with greenhouse gas emission cuts and achieving sustainable development goals for something that was more 'business as usual'?

As ever, my answer was 'no, sorry (and also not sorry).' My business that morning was to champion the end of the linear extractive model of take-make-waste that governs our consumer existence and the way we do business on this planet. The linear system is, as you are no doubt aware, a reckless, short-term quasi-system that wreaks havoc on our planet. The goods and services we produce and consume at speed are undermining our very existence on planet Earth and we are taking out an unprecedented number of other species too. Nothing less than the wholesale shift to a new circular economy model that would design out waste forever and unlock a whole raft of benefits, including a drastic cut in greenhouse gas emissions, will do. But in the end, during this panel, we ended up squabbling over cucumbers; some packagers demanding the right to carry on wrapping them in single use plastic.

Diving into a near completed version of this book provided the perfect antidote. Sangeeta sees the bigger picture for sure and is not afraid of provocation (as the title of this book shows). But her great gift is being able to synthesize her encyclopaedic knowledge of CSR and her close observations in very useful and clear language. Within these pages, Sangeeta gives radical-yet-precise action meaning. But she never forgets the fundamentals, including the mandate for change from the global public and, unlike so many books on this subject, she maintains a global outlook, taking the temperature of the growth of CSR in different territories – the chapter on India was particularly useful for me.

Sangeeta is a generous author, who passes the microphone naturally and judiciously. This book is also filled with unique and different global business voices, questioned with precision to get their perspectives on how we can get the type of transformational change we need.

They are the voices of now, including David Katz from Plastic Bank, but you also get a sense of the history and richness of CSR; through Loïs Acton for example, we also hear her mentor, the late Dame Anita Roddick.

This book comes at a point when brands and industries have woken up to CSR and moved from 'mindlessly operating around the tactical' to 'questioning the very reason why something is being done.' That would have represented a great moment to publish this book in and of itself, but then came COVID-19. Hats off to Sangeeta who also weaves in a thoughtful response to the global pandemic and deftly explains the part CSR can and must play from hereon in. "The virus has touched all of humanity and, as happens at moments of great change, we will emerge with new clarity about our systems – political, economic, social and ecological. We're gaining new insight into what's strong, what's weak, what's corrupt, what matters and what doesn't," she writes as she helps us navigate this collective experience.

I hesitate to be too prescriptive when writing a foreword; each of us gets different things from the same piece of work. But what I emerged with by the end of this book was a greater confidence in my own mission-led approach when dealing with business and industries across sectors. I learned about the mechanics of good CSR and how those mechanisms deliver on climate goals or resource use. I also felt that I had met a whole community of CEOs, led by Sangeeta, who were all pulling in the same direction. At that point I felt both supported and empowered. I hope you will join us!

Lucy Siegle
November 2020

Introduction

THE
TIPPING
POINT

In January 2020, I intuitively felt that I had to write this book because it was apparent that businesses needed to change to do better, if we as a planet were to survive. The COVID-19 pandemic had not hit us yet, but it was already clear that we were at a tipping point due to climate change and so many other sustainability issues. We had alarm warnings from the United Nations (UN), scientists and Sir David Attenborough about how the world is fighting a battle against plastic pollution; unsustainable fashion and beauty; climate changes caused by rising CO2 emissions; the rapid disappearance of the Amazon forests; extinction of species; the environmental impact of palm oil production; and so much more. The list is endless.

We began 2020 with the bush fires in Australia taking place in January. By March the virus had struck, and then we had the rise of the Black Lives Matter (BLM) movement in May, sparked by the death of African American George Floyd at the hands of the Minneapolis police. Huge protests took place across the US and Europe against racism and the police killings of black Americans. These three big news events impacted local communities, global societies and businesses. Before the conversations around race, diversity and inclusion blew up, I had included the need for ethnic diversity in business in chapters two and seven of this book. While writing, I revisited these points to ensure that I do justice to this important issue.

When I started to write this book, the planet was entering a state of global emergency, battling the deadly COVID-19 pandemic. In less than a week, lives all over the world had changed. Our worlds became complex and chaotic, as we waged war with this invisible enemy. Schools closed and supermarket shelves ran empty as people stockpiled. Toilet rolls became gold, people worked from home and telecom companies experienced surges in internet use and collaboration apps. Now, self-isolating and social distancing are now firmly part of our vocabulary. Oh, and we no longer shake hands. We were all in a surreal Hollywood blockbuster, with no superhero to save us. The planet was in lockdown.

It became clear to me that this book was needed for all the small- to medium-sized companies, start-ups and entrepreneurs, because consumers have changed in what they want and need. People want all businesses to do better! Consumers have been closely watching how businesses are behaving during this global pandemic, and those companies that have proved to be real heroes will find that the goodwill towards their brand lasts. There is going to be growth in people wanting and buying brands that reflect their values. We've already seen that this crisis has changed the mindset of some businesses, which have pivoted to truly step up and deliver.

I wanted to write a book that was different – one that would convey that we should all be doing better. I wanted to show business owners how they can easily bring about the changes that this planet so desperately needs. We all can learn from others, especially through the power of stories. To that end, I have gathered a set of unique and different global business voices, who offer their perspectives on how CEOs can lead businesses to do things better, with profit. These 'conversation pieces' include David Katz from Plastic Bank and a very special interview with Loïs Acton, who was mentored by the late Dame Anita Roddick. I know you'll enjoy reading these conversations as much as I enjoyed interviewing these insightful minds. I trust you'll find that none of these interviews disappoint; they are gritty and authentic. Each one will make you think.

I have also written a chapter about India, because I think the West can learn a lot from the East. That's particularly true of developing economies, which have always had sustainability at the heart of their communities but, with globalization, have become lost.

As companies have emerged from lockdowns, into worldwide economic uncertainty, we have seen that sustainable brands have outperformed conventional ones. Businesses continue to fight for survival and have acknowledged that corporate social responsibility (CSR) can be an important part of recovery, because we'll remember those companies that stepped up to lead in 2020 and beyond.

This book, with its inspiring real-life stories and trends from around the world, is for big and small brands – both new and established companies – that want to do good. Its main message is that, to drive sustainability, businesses need to position that priority, along with diversity and inclusion, at the heart of their brand.

BRANDS THAT STEPPED UP DURING COVID-19

We have witnessed certain businesses and organizations around the globe acting quickly, with 'brand kindness.' This has involved creating funds for consumers and businesses in need, alleviating employee hardships, providing food for children who depend on school for meals, and more. These actions came from a wide variety of sectors. We had Pret a Manger sandwich shoppes give free drinks to front-line health workers from the UK's National Health Service (NHS). LinkedIn opened up its learning courses for free, using its platform to share news more broadly, help businesses use live video to replace in-person events and deal with business continuity.

The world of fashion did its bit too. The shoe retailer Kurt Geiger launched 'Small Acts of Kindness,' closing its high street stores across UK and Ireland and urging employees to use their paid leave to become part of the neighbourly volunteering scheme launched by Age UK. The brand also leveraged the campaign across its social media channels, with store managers donating £100 gift cards to 55 NHS critical care workers in each of their local hospitals. The retailer's chief executive, Neil Clifford, personally donated gift cards at the Queen Alexandra Hospital in Portsmouth. Meanwhile, contemporary French label Zadig & Voltaire supported the Paris Hospital Foundations, donating 20% of sales of its new collection sold via its online store in France.

Luxury brands also played their part. Prada, a big fashion brand, turned its production lines from creating beautiful blouses to producing 110,000 masks. The fashion house Gucci said it would make more than a million masks, and Yves Saint Laurent and Balenciaga – both of which, like Gucci, are owned by Kering – manufactured them. LVMH Moët Hennessy, the French company behind major brands like Louis Vuitton, Fenty Beauty and Benefit Cosmetics, announced that its factories that normally produce perfume would manufacture hand sanitizer gel and deliver it to French healthcare authorities for free.

High street brands shifted their focus too. Spanish-owned Zara, which pledged to produce surgical masks, said it had donated 10,000 masks, and the H&M Group said it would rearrange its supply chain to produce protective equipment for hospitals and healthcare workers. Even the global bridal brand Pronovias showed its support by donating wedding dresses to front-line hospital worker brides-to-be. The initiative started in China earlier in 2020, where the company provided many nurses and doctors with wedding gowns before extending the initiative to hospital employees worldwide.

UK gas and electricity suppliers rolled out an emergency package of measures to ensure that vulnerable people didn't get cut off during the outbreak. We even saw former British footballers Gary Neville and Ryan Giggs open their hotels to NHS workers, free of charge. In the US, with the disruption of in-person sports seasons, the major football, basketball and hockey leagues offered free viewing of certain programming. For example, the National Football League offered free access to its NFL Game Pass broadcast package, and included access to past regular and postseason games. Basketball fans received a free preview of NBA League Pass.

Starbucks decided to delay the expiration of its 'Star' loyalty programme member points until 1 June 2020. Facebook offered $100 million in cash grants and credits to up to 30,000 eligible small businesses in 20 countries. Amazon launched the AWS Diagnostic Development Initiative to support its customers working on diagnostic R&D, and has initially invested $20 million. IKEA donated 50,000 facemasks that it found in a furniture warehouse in Sweden.

Companies have led the way in demonstrating kindness and humanity, showing that there is a better way to do business. Small- to medium-sized businesses are the backbone of most economies around the world, where they are often able to be more innovative than larger organizations, implementing ideas faster and pivoting easier than many big companies. Their response to the virus reflected that flexibility and nimbleness.

Many brands won't make it through the economic bloodbath that lies ahead. Those that do survive will be an inspiration to us all, showing that a great revolution in business is coming. It will be a sea change that will wash away both the bad actors and the average companies that are watching lazily from the sidelines and reacting indifferently. Those brands – along with their PR teams and marketers, who don't get their act together and try to understand the human on the other side – will find it tough to survive.

Prior to this moment, many brands and industries were mindlessly operating around the tactical, rather than questioning the very reason why something is being done. A UK survey[1] commissioned by the Royal Society of Arts and The Food Foundation in April 2020 showed that there's a real appetite for change. Only 9% of Britons want life to return to 'normal' after the coronavirus outbreak is over. People noticed significant changes during the lockdown, including cleaner air, more wildlife and stronger communities. More than half (54%) of 4,343 people who participated in a UK YouGov poll said they hoped to make changes in their own lives, and for the country as a whole, to learn from the crisis.

This is where small- and medium-sized businesses come in, as they can innovate for change and integrate real CSR initiatives into the heart of their brands and companies. It has become important for brands to communicate authentically, compassionately and personally. Sincerity and authenticity are critical, and that's not an entirely new notion. PR experts like myself have been saying this for years, because we've always known that consumers have a keen ability to filter out opportunistic hype. COVID-19 has not been a marketing opportunity to capitalize on, but instead a time to understand the unique role a brand plays in people's lives and how this may have changed under these circumstances. All types of companies and organizations have had to immediately understand the unprecedented new problems facing consumers, and find solutions. They've had to show sensitivity and empathy in communicating with consumers.

The pandemic has shown us that no one can prosper alone, and that we've all been impacted by it. We have been fully awakened to the fact that we are a connected world offline, where this virus has transcended all borders and socio-economic distinctions. The health of the planet was put first. At a time when we needed more global collaboration, many of our political leaders did not rise to the challenge, but many businesses did! In recent years, businesses have shown a greater understanding about connecting the dots and working collectively, though a thriving society and planet is still light years away.

THE PLANETARY ISSUES BEFORE COVID-19 STILL EXIST

In 2019, the UN voiced concerns that the world was off-course in its attempts to mitigate the global climate-change crisis, as greenhouse gas emissions and global temperatures continued to rise. Scientific data has shown that the last four years have been the hottest on record, and winter temperatures in the Arctic have risen by 3°C since 1990. Sea levels are rising, coral reefs are dying, and we're starting to see the life-threatening impact of climate change on health, through air pollution, heat waves and threats to food security. If that wasn't enough, the planet is choking with plastic. Surfers Against Sewage, a UK marine conservation charity, estimates that every day approximately eight million pieces of plastic pollution find their way into our oceans.

In 2015, US President Barack Obama stated, "No challenge poses a greater threat to future generations than climate change," in his State of the Union address.[2] In 2019, Mark Carney, the governor of the Bank of England, gave a stark warning to businesses in an interview with *The Guardian* newspaper. He warned that "firms ignoring climate crisis will go bankrupt." He went on to say that disclosure by companies of the risks posed by climate change to their business was key to a smooth transition to a zero-carbon world, as it enabled investors to back winners. He said certain industries, sectors and firms would do very well during this process because they'll be part of the solution. However, there would also be ones that lag behind, and they will be punished.

Prior to COVID-19, consumers already supported a change of attitude that put sustainability at the heart of a brand, to ensure that business is done differently. For years, CSR has been one arm of a brand/business; a small component to do good and support causes. It has been a function that's resided in either human resources, marketing or internal communications. It has also been a function that, at times, had no budget or was a line item in another group's budget.

Companies and organizations are recognizing that to have credibility – to endure as a brand and remain relevant – they need a holistic approach to their CSR values. They've also come to realize that CSR must sit within the business strategy, not outside of it. Now, more than ever, businesses are expected to have a position on political, environmental and social issues. However, engaging on these weighty issues can seem tricky, and even risky. While brands must stand for something, because consumers want and demand it, they must also live it, and this is why that commitment needs to be integrated into the core business strategy.

In the modern marketplace, CSR initiatives provide the most powerful differentiating factor for businesses. They point the way forward to doing business better and deliver whole range of benefits, from recruiting the best talent and employee retention to word-of-mouth popularity, customer loyalty and profit. Consumers across generations and countries are demanding that businesses contribute more to society and the planet. They are alert to empty platitudes and want real, meaningful change.

NOW IS THE TIME FOR CSR

Therefore, with everything that's happening in the world, there has never been a better time for all types of brands and organizations to rethink their purpose and what they represent. Those businesses that have been able to quickly act, and show empathy through their CSR values, have added long-term value to their brands.

Historically, CSR activities have been about charitable giving and helping local communities, supporting schools, assisting the homeless, raising funds for local charities, etc. But in today's world, CSR is an integral part of how a company operates. There is a need for companies to demonstrate what they are doing as part of their business for customers, employees and society at large. CSR is a business value, where organizations and companies integrate social and environmental concerns into their business operations and interactions with stakeholders. It is a way to generate a balance of economic, environmental and social objectives, which is also known as the 'Triple Bottom Line.' This is the notion that instead of one purely 'dollars and cents' bottom line, there should be three: profit, people and the planet.

Over the last 20 years we've seen some companies promote their CSR values and initiatives, spotlighting how their business relates to the environment and society. However, being a socially responsible business is not just about implementing a set of environmental and social objectives. It's much more than this and, to get it right, it must be able to brave any degree of public and media scrutiny. It is a mindset – a fundamental commitment to do business differently. It's also an evolving business practice, which will always create a positive impact and motivate you as a business owner.

CSR goes beyond the legal and compliance obligations of good governance; it's about putting social and environmental concerns at the heart of their businesses for sustainable, long-term gains. It is a way of doing business better that should sit at the core of your company, woven into the fabric of your brand and part of every decision that's made. It is not about image or about 'seen to be doing good.' Why? Because the costs of only paying lip service to your business CSR commitment is a risky proposition that could just cost you, your business and brand. This is especially true as we know that today's consumers and employees are savvy and able to sniff out anything that is fake. Moreover, social media has put everything under a relentless, 24/7 spotlight.

Investing to become a sustainable business can be a little more expensive, but the long-term returns on investment will be high. That's true not just in terms of profit, but for your employees, the wider community around you and ultimately the little bit of the planet where you run your business. Our human relationships as a business demand that we do things differently, and be more thoughtful and sustainable in our approaches. Natural resources are running out, and the safety and security of the world itself is increasingly precarious.

Being a sustainably-led business enhances the karmic relationship between your company and the Earth, and when you view it this way, it's much easier to integrate your CSR initiatives into your business strategy.

Chapter 1

WHAT IS CSR AND WHY IS IT IMPORTANT?

I am sure many of us have heard the term CSR and have our own interpretation of what it means.

The UN describes it as "a management concept whereby companies integrate social and environmental concerns in their business operations and interactions with their stakeholders. CSR is generally understood as being the way through which a company achieves a balance of economic, environmental and social imperatives ('Triple-Bottom-Line Approach'), while at the same time addressing the expectations of shareholders and stakeholders."

In other words, it is a company's fundamental societal responsibility, as its decisions and activities clearly have an impact on society and the environment. Socially-responsible companies' transparent, ethical behaviour contributes in a positive way to sustainable development, including the health and the welfare of society.

However, it is also important to draw a distinction between CSR, which is a strategic business management concept, and the broader realm of philanthropy, not-for-profits and charities. CSR enhances the reputation of a company and strengthens the brand.

Now, more than ever, businesses are putting CSR at the heart of their strategies because they can see the inherent business benefits, and because they sincerely want to make a difference.

BUSINESS BENEFITS OF CSR

Running a business is always about making a profit, and over the course of this book you'll learn from the interviews I conducted with business leaders and change-makers that being a CSR-led business can be profitable.

The impact of CSR on a company's performance has become an important issue for its investors and management. As a result, many businesses across different sectors have begun to publicly report CSR-related activities to show their interest, investment and commitment to society. They are also interested in better monitoring and measuring their social responsibility activities. A company with strong CSR values will have a high degree of transparency and enjoy greater trust, which will be naturally attractive to consumers and employees. This also means the senior management team understands the value of non-financial issues to a company's valuation.

Over the years, the relationship between CSR and financial performance has been studied in different ways, and many researchers have found that there's a positive connection.[3] However, it's also true that some research claims to show a negative relationship between these two factors,[4] and other studies argue that there's no connection at all.[5]

But, of course, everything is about proof and actions. The world's largest investment management firm, Black-Rock, announced in early 2020 that it's making climate change the company's top priority moving forward. Chairman and CEO Larry Fink believes that we're on the verge of a fundamental reshaping of finance, and said that sustainability will become BlackRock's new standard for investing. "Climate risk is investment risk," he said.

"Indeed, climate change is almost invariably the top issue that clients around the world raise."[6]

BlackRock is not the only company that realizes how rapidly environmental awareness is changing. Major investors on an international level are increasingly using positive screening, and disinvesting from companies that fail to meet the expected environmental, social and governance (ESG) criteria. ESG refers to a class of investing also known as 'sustainable investing.' This umbrella term covers three main factors: 'E' is for 'environment,' and includes issues such as climate change policies, carbon footprint and use of renewable energies; 'S' is for 'social,' and includes workers' rights and protections; and 'G' is for 'governance,' and includes boardroom diversity and corporate transparency.

The number of indices and tracker funds that play into the ESG theme is rapidly growing, with data providers advising companies of their ESG scores, so investment and fund managers can assess whether to invest in them. For instance, luxury fashion house Prada is implementing sustainable practices and has created a €50 million, five-year sustainability term loan with Crédit Agricole Group. The agreement allows for the interest rates to be adjusted annually, if three sustainability targets are met. These are:

1. A certain number of stores receive an LEED Gold or Platinum certification

2. Employees achieve a set number of training hours

3. Targets are met for using a sustainable nylon substitute in the production of goods

These three objectives were chosen by Crédit Agricole from a list provided by Prada, which prioritized targets that support artisanship, energy savings and 'circularity,' an economic model aimed at eliminating waste and decreasing the use of limited resources. The loan is the latest in a series of sustainable initiatives undertaken in 2019 by Prada, which also owns Miu Miu, Church's and Car Shoe.

Prada's initiative is the first of its kind in the luxury goods industry, and now similar loans are being implemented elsewhere. According to data from the news and analysis service Environmental Finance, the sustainability-linked loan market has grown from $5 billion in 2017 to $40 billion in 2018.[7] And now that luxury consumer brands have increased their sustainability-linked loans, a lot of other companies are expected to follow suit. For certain sectors, like oil, gas and mining, the theme of sustainability has been a lot more pressing, and Crédit Agricole has extended sustainability loans to entities like natural gas producers.

I believe CSR can effortlessly improve profits. When a business or brand puts sustainability authentically at the centre of its business and strategy, it will automatically gain respect in the marketplace. This in turn will generate positive word-of-mouth, influence higher sales, enhance employee loyalty and attract better talent. CSR activities that focus on sustainability issues can lower costs and improve efficiencies in the long term. An added advantage for public companies is that CSR activities can help them gain a listing in the FTSE4Good, Dow Jones Sustainability Indices or other trackers, which can enhance the company's stock price, boosting executives' compensation and making shareholders happier.

There is enough proof that when your CSR initiatives are set, and are firmly integrated with your brand values and business strategy, they help a business create the right kind of partnerships and collaborations. Sustainable business values act as a moral compass, enhancing trust with your workforce and fostering brand loyalty with your customers. If your firm is thinking of entering into a partnership and the other party doesn't have any authentic, core CSR values, they won't be aligned with your overall business objectives and any collaboration poses a risk to your brand. For example, they could have a high carbon footprint, or have poor employee practices, or don't believe in reducing their plastic use. Whatever it is, this type of organization has the potential to upset your existing and potential customers, and mar your reputation.

Nigel Green, CEO of the financial consultancy deVere Group, predicts that the economic fallout of the coronavirus pandemic will trigger a 'skyward surge' in sustainable, responsible and impactful investing over the next 12 months. He cites three key reasons:

1. Before the pandemic, research revealed that investments that score well in terms of ESG credentials often outperform the market and have lower volatility over the long run. Since the COVID-19 public health emergency upended the world, the latest broad analysis shows that ESG funds have typically continued to outperform others.

2. The pandemic has underscored the vulnerability and fragility of societies, and the planet as a whole. In its wake, companies will only survive and thrive if they operate with a nod from the wider court of public approval. The crisis has highlighted the complexity and interconnectedness of our world in terms of demand and supply, and every aspect of trade and commerce, and how these can be under threat if not sustainably managed.

3. Demographic shifts will support the trend. Millennials, who were born between the early 1980s and the late '90s are keenly focused on ESG. In fact, a global survey conducted by the deVere Group in January 2020 revealed that 77% of millennials said ESG was their top priority when considering investment opportunities.[8] This is crucial because the biggest-ever generational transfer of wealth – likely to be around $30 trillion worldwide, passing from baby boomers to millennials – will take place in the next few years.

Green put it this way: "ESG investing was already going to reshape the investment landscape in this new decade, but the coronavirus will quicken the pace of this reshaping. Investors are increasingly aware that it is possible – and increasingly necessary – to make a profit while positively and proactively protecting people and the planet. They will be making investment decisions after measuring the sustainability and societal impact of a sector or company, as these criteria help to better determine their future financial performance: in other words, their risk and return."[9]

BUILDING CSR INTO YOUR BUSINESS STRATEGY

Nothing about creating a sustainable business should be complicated; the principles are easy enough to get a handle on and successfully execute. It's important that CSR initiatives and values go beyond 'doing good' and that they aim to tell a company's story, which is very much part of the brand story.

Your CSR values need to connect to the organization's core business purpose and strategy in a way that makes intuitive sense. Your business can create an effective corporate social responsibility programme that is strategic and sustainable using these seven simple steps:

1. **Build Your Strategy Around Your Company's Core Competencies.** There are many worthy causes a company can choose to support but, without focus and alignment with what your business already does, the chosen CSR efforts will not be effective. If a company has strengths, research and knowledge in a specific area, supporting a project that aligns with that expertise can help generate new customer visibility and revenue streams.

2. **Develop CSR Initiatives That Align With Your Workforce.** Strategic companies are using CSR programmes to protect and grow their most valuable asset: their employees. Millennials generally consider a company's social and environmental commitments when deciding where to work. At the same time, engaged employees are more likely to stay with a company longer, reducing attrition costs and the associated disruption.

3. Get Buy-In From All. From bottom to top and top to bottom, everyone in the organization has to be 'in' and an active participant. That means the entire workforce, including the C-suite. CSR needs to be firmly embedded in the culture of the organization before launching any programmes. This makes the engagement meaningful and helps employees understand the full business process, which then creates an emotional bond for both clients and staff.

4. Recognize Issues That Matter To Your Customers. Your customers care about what you're doing and will reward socially responsible companies through brand loyalty. Media coverage of business scandals has shown that consumers will boycott or otherwise punish companies that have acted irresponsibly or harmfully, often using the power of social media to voice their outrage.

5. Measure The Return On Investment Of Your CSR Efforts, For Management And Investors. Measuring CSR programmes is only difficult when initiatives span different departments, such as communications, marketing, human resources and compliance. Instead, develop and create a holistic approach – an organized, integrated framework for reporting to investors. Quantify socially conscious efforts that are directly tied to the company's bottom line.

6. Strong, Sustainable Partnerships Breed Success. Partnerships let you draw on the capabilities of other networks that have expertise in different fields. Connecting with partners who have the same values can help you develop thoughtful CSR initiatives faster and more affordably than trying to create opportunities on your own.

7. **Find New Drivers Of Innovation.** Companies can use CSR as an innovation driver, investing in initiatives for research, development and implementation. This will continually bring new information into the process, and it helps keep the work close to the market.

IN CONVERSATION... WITH MARK DODD

In April 2020, I spoke with Mark Dodd, Financial Planner and Partner at the award-winning firm Holden and Partners, specialists in ethical, sustainable and thematic investment. Here's what we discussed:

1. **What does sustainable investing mean and why is it important?**
It is the ability of companies to ensure the longevity of their products, processes and business models and is the responsibility of all types of businesses, irrespective of sectors they operate in – to deliver sustainable business practices and products back to the world, with a holistic approach to how they operate. Across business, there is big change happening, including with those companies that haven't historically subscribed to this way of operating. They're increasingly now seeing the value of doing so, both to them financially and the environment.

The examples I always like to use with my clients are the extractive industries like oil, mining and mineral/resource extraction, many of whom would fail abysmally in the criteria used to assess them in an environmental, sustainability and governance approach. Whilst I understand that companies like Shell and BP are now looking to build wind farms and are moving into renewable energy sectors, they're doing so because of public and market pressures, where we as individuals want businesses that we're buying services from to operate more ethically and sustainably.

At the same time, companies realize that this need to be sustainable is growing, and if they don't change they will miss out altogether. In order to survive, they need to change their business models.

It is really driven by everyone, and that includes the media.

2. **What changes have you seen in the last ten years regarding ethical investment?**
A move from negative to positive screening.

3. **What does screening mean?**
It is scrutinizing companies that are held in investment funds, to see what they actually do and what strategies they apply. It sifts out companies that are involved in the production of armaments, tobacco and pornography – those sort of classic, old-school industries and methods of assessment. The screening filters out those companies operating in these types of spaces, throws the spotlight on those with a positive approach, and selects investments because

they do good. So, I come back to renewable energy as an example, where we look at funds holding companies operating in this space. Another one is extraction industries, who are now generating their incomes from other sources that would fit into a much more positive view of their activities.

We look at the good things that companies are doing rather than the bad. It is a change in investor attitude to where they are investing.

4. What, or who, is driving the change?

This change is being driven by the media, by advisors like ourselves who actively promote this type of investment and, as we strive to get our messaging out to a wider audience, more and more of our clients will subscribe to it.

The ethos at Holden and Partners has been set on these sustainable principles from day one, but the landscape has changed dramatically. It is about education, where you're educating your clients on the things that they can do, based on their investment decisions that are positive to the environment, which don't have a negative impact on their own financial outcomes.

Over the years we have been able to demonstrate that the maturity of what I will loosely call 'ethical investing' has got to the point where there are some genuine, positive stories around the outcomes. Maybe ten years ago these were harder to find, where the investment options were more limited. Now, what's happening is that more and more people are looking at this and asking these questions of investment managers, who are then starting to ask these questions of the managers that they're investing in. It starts to snowball from there.

5. What kind of growth has there been over the last ten years? Have the regulators encouraged more of an ethical investment approach?

There has been significant growth in those offering advice on investment solutions, where a move towards ethical investing has become the core investment approach.

There is some evidence of the regulators becoming involved, including suggestions to the trustees of charities, and trustees of large pension schemes, to consider investing ethically. So, yes, I think the regulator has a part to play in it.

6. Do clients want to make more of a conscious difference when investing?

Yes, increasingly so. It started with younger investors, who are now encouraging their parents to consider this approach, and the driver is education.

Younger clients are looking to invest and wouldn't think twice about investing in an ethically screened portfolio. What we are finding, along with other firms, is that we have client relationships along the lines of a family structure, and families talk. Plus, kids are not afraid to pull their parents up if they think where they are investing is wrong. So, where families are talking about finances, we are finding that the messaging coming out from children is one where they are encouraging their parents to change their views on how to invest. These children are saying we need to save the environment for our grandchildren and that message is filtering down to their parents, who are now starting, in our view, to change some of their views on the importance of this style of investment.

And while I suspect that some parents have never given it a great deal of thought, for many of our clients that's not the case, as we advise many who have been investing in this way for a long time.

7. **Could the fund management industry be doing more to encourage sustainable investing?**
Everyone can, though care is needed to correctly identify those who are genuine and those who are just jumping on the bandwagon.

8. **So, how does Holden and Partners differentiate between those who are genuine and those who jump on the bandwagon?**
Interesting question. It's '*do your research*.' It's to look back at the behaviour of managers before, and when this change came about. We devolve to our investment managers to do this level of research. They then go and talk to the (business) managers and look them in the eye. They can tell if someone is just jumping on this, and you also just know who are companies that have been involved in this space for a long time. Even with how things have changed now, with more remote meetings, you can still get a sense of someone's honesty.

It's not overly difficult for our investment managers to say that this is genuine or that this is a company that has come to this very late – with no track record, and isn't showing other signs of making changes to their business that would demonstrate that they are taking things seriously.

9. **What is thematic investing and how do you identify themes? Can you give an example of the type of opportunities you've identified?**

It is identifying global macroeconomic themes and seeking out investment opportunities that are best placed to capitalize upon them. Some of the themes are fairly simple to identify and others are a little more challenging.

The one I like to look at is the 'grey population.' That's the growing number of the elderly in our world, who have a different set of demands than a younger population. Where there are companies developing products that meet the needs of this older demographic, as opposed to the requirements of the younger generation – those are really interesting themes. Although the younger generation have been driving the sustainable conversation, the older generation are also changing their thinking, where perhaps they were more concerned about what they need, such as different clothing, different medical facilities, different equipment to run their homes. But actually, they are starting to, in my view, look at the longer term of the impact of the environment and how it would affect their children and their children's grandchildren, if they don't start to change.

Other themes are addressing agricultural production and food or water scarcity, for example. These types of themes become more important as conversations develop.

10. **What do you think the future looks like for ethical, sustainable and thematic investing?**

It's THE future of investing.

11. **Will loyalty still be important to the next generation, who have inherited their parents' wealth, for
ethical investing?**
It has challenges. And the dynamics of this is that
in the main, they don't have funds to invest, though
what we and most sensible businesses would do is
look at a wider succession planning strategy, where
we engage with all members of a family across the
age spectrum. That starts with the parents, or
possibly the grandparents, who are the key custodians of the family assets, right through to their
children or grandchildren, where our involvement
starts with basic financial education and developing financial independence from their parents. We
look to be delivering a financial education to that
next generation, because they're going to be the
next custodians of the assets. The key relationship
would remain with the parents or grandparents,
who will realistically continue to hold the keys to
the family wealth.

12. **Do you think the COVID-19 pandemic will change
how people invest their wealth?**
During lockdown we were all acutely aware that the
levels of pollution had reduced and that air quality
improved massively. But as we have moved out of
lockdown, some things have gone back to normal,
like the litter throwing. I think there's a view that we
don't need to return to the rat race, the daily com-
mute on packed public transport, sitting in offices in
city centre areas, and that companies have demonstrated they can work in this new way, which will
have big, longer-term benefits to the environment.

We as a company adapted quite easily to this new way of operating and working from home. You've got to plan for your business, which we had, and therefore it wasn't difficult for us to transition.

We also have the right infrastructure to support us – the right IT and support. We started to work from home two weeks before the government asked us to, as we could see what was coming and wanted to reduce the risks to our staff. We could see it was best to keep our staff safe. The origin of our business is based on ethical values, which has helped us build our identity and has relevance to the thinking of how we believe we should deliver services and solutions to our clients.

I see the challenges, though less so for smaller businesses, who are more agile and innovative, to deliver on issues like this. But, with what's been going on with COVID-19, we have seen some smaller businesses struggle. We could see more of government-run organizations, something akin to nationalization, that won't be able to deliver in the same way as smaller businesses. Companies' ability to survive is the biggest question out there.

In my view, I believe this pandemic will have an impact for a long time, an impact that could last at least 100 years, where it could take our children's generation and our grandchildren's generation to recover from this financially. The amount of money being created by governments around the world is so astronomical that it is so difficult to understand how it will ever be repaid.

The coronavirus has made us have these deep thoughts. We are questioning what the world might look like.

So, while it is doing good things for the planet – like the reduction in travel and mining – at the same time, the financial implications are huge and I don't think they were being considered at the early stages of the pandemic.

THE BODY SHOP: AN AVANT-GARDE APPROACH TO CSR

The Body Shop is one great example of putting CSR at the heart of a business.

Founded by Dame Anita Roddick in 1976, this cosmetics, skin care and perfume brand was built on the principles of CSR. The idea that a company could make money and be a force for good was laughed at 40 years ago, when Roddick set up the business. But now, her pioneering philosophy is mainstream, with many international brands putting sustainability at the centre of their business. Her pioneering approach has contributed greatly to the rise of the CSR formula.

In the '80s, The Body Shop was offering customers the option to recycle their empty plastic bottles in-store or refill used containers. In 2020, global consumers are demanding that supermarkets and retailers offer this sort of service, due to the pressing need to reduce plastic and waste. While Roddick's stand against animal testing challenged the whole cosmetics industry to make changes – and ultimately led to a European ban – vegan beauty brands and products are now big business.

When The Body Shop celebrated its 40th birthday in 2016, it launched a global CSR strategy to unify its message: 'Enrich Not Exploit.' The aim was to support the company's goal to become the world's most ethical and sustainable global business. It echoes Roddick's belief that business could be 'a force for good.' The company was acquired by L'Oréal in 2006, but has stayed true to its roots by keeping social and environmental issues top-of-mind through urgent, compelling campaigns. The 'Enrich Not Exploit' commitment has taken this one step further, ensuring that CSR is incorporated into all business decisions, while holding the company accountable through specific, measureable goals.

IN CONVERSATION... WITH LOÏS ACTON

I first met Loïs Acton at the March 2020 Green Events & Innovations Conference, organized by A Greener Festival, a non-profit group dedicated to helping events and venues become greener. She was a featured speaker, and during her talk mentioned that she'd been mentored by Anita Roddick. I knew then that I needed Loïs' story for the book, and I was lucky enough to have that conversation with her in June 2020. I think you'll agree after reading this dialogue that Loïs' and Anita's lives kept crisscrossing, were full of serendipity, and it seems that destiny brought them together.

Loïs is purposeful and passionate, dedicating her life to positive change and campaigning for social justice through music and the arts. She started her career teaching, and in the 1970s founded one of the first real free schools in the UK.

She moved into British TV, working on a variety of programmes and groundbreaking initiatives. Her work at ITV included the launch of the MOBO Awards, the TV Diversity and Disability Networks, Carlton TV's support for the CRE Race in the Media Awards, the EMMAs and the Carlton TV Trust. She helped set up the award-winning Carlton/ITV social programming unit, helped develop the Missing Persons charity and the Community Channel, and sat on various boards, including that of Crimestoppers. She also assisted on Channel 4's White Room music series and worked at the Glastonbury Festival for many years.

When Loïs left ITV after 14 years, one of the many important and successful things she did was to found Urban Unlimited and the UUNetwork, bringing grassroots creativity from traditionally excluded backgrounds into the creative industries.

1. **How did you meet Anita Roddick and how did she become your mentor? What was it like to be mentored by Anita?**

I would like to start a little further back, because it's really important. And when I did meet Anita again, it is something that I had to tell her. I had a difficult situation to deal with, as most of us do, and in the 70s I went to stay with my mother with my two young children. I was very down and depressed, and on an awful rainy day, I decided to take the children out. They were under my mother's feet, so we went to a local bus stop to get a bus to Littlehampton. At the bus stop, an estate car pulled up, the window went down and the driver asked if we would like a lift. We got into the car with this woman, and on our journey the woman was very excited and I forgot all my problems. She was telling me about her new shop that she had opened, that it was her first shop, and it was all big adventure. That woman was Anita Roddick.

I remembered what she told me, and it was a few years later that I realized that the shop the woman told me about was The Body Shop. In my own personal career, I had set up something called the Bermondsey Lamppost, a free school working with street kids. It was an organization that I set up while being a teacher. I strongly believe that acts of kindness really affect us, and Anita's act of kindness affected me from that first moment.

It was only when I was at ITV that our paths crossed again; I had now become a producer/director and a senior researcher, with a remit looking at social issues. We were looking at housing, education, crime, health – you name it, we did it! With my boss, we discussed two projects that we could help develop using television: one was Missing Persons and the other was Crimestoppers. I eventually went on to become a vice-patron of Missing Persons, a charity that I helped develop, and was also on the board of Crimestoppers. Amazingly, one of the first companies to come on board with Missing Persons was The Body Shop; their lorries carried the first photos of Missing Persons. I then met with Jilly Forster, Anita's best friend, who did the PR for The Body Shop.

We now cut away to 2006. I had left ITV in 2004, and a board member loved what I was doing with regards to the social projects that I had developed and nurtured outside of ITV, where we had filmed a lot of them. Consequently, ITV gave me an office for another few years, based on what I do now. I founded Urban Unlimited and the UUNetwork to develop links between the creative industries and grassroots creativity from traditionally excluded backgrounds. In March 2006, the British Library set up the 'Business and IP Centre,' supporting business owners, inventors, entrepreneurs and SMEs (small- and medium-sized enterprises). I went along at that time and won a bid to be mentored, and the person I bid to be my mentor was Anita Roddick.

I set out the reasons why I wanted Anita as my mentor, and why the project would be relevant and of interest to her. And I won a whole day with Anita, including follow-up with her, and that experience was amazing. Obviously, I had to tell her that she had influenced me from the time she picked me up from that bus stop! What was special for me was that I had watched The Body Shop grow from that one shop in Chichester to where she was now, looking for a second property.

When we met the second time, through the British Library, I showed Anita all the different projects and why I felt that, joined up, our thinking was important. And what was extraordinary for me was that Anita got exactly what I was talking about and what I wanted to achieve. I haven't met anyone else who has really gelled with understanding what's in my head, in terms of grassroots. Ordinary people make a contribution to life that is not recognized, and kindness and generosity are as important in a company as in a grassroots organization.

During my mentoring session that day, we looked at plans and ways forward, and Anita said, "Look, I want my company to help you, I want to come on board and I want you to meet my MD, and for him to help you." In a way, the way she sourced her supply chain and procurement is very similar to what we are talking about in the creative industries. It's how you knit that together with the end product. We had a wonderful day together.

2. How did your relationship inspire you to work differently?

Anita gave me a copy of her book, *Business As Unusual*, and if anybody hasn't read it, I highly recommend it.[10] In her introduction, Anita says that what she wanted to achieve was a "revolution in kindness" and that "treating people properly in companies, from their employees to their markets, would be better for the soul."

I too was able to give back to the British Library later. And just to go a little further, I met Anita in 2006 and she died in 2007. In that six months to a year that I had with Anita, I spent time with her in her London flat and with her MD, Peter Tyson, who I still keep in touch with. On September 9 2007, I was part of a procession in Soho with Emma Thompson, Anita's daughter Sam Roddick and a whole host of other women creating public awareness for the sex trafficking campaign. The very next day Anita passed away. It was devastating and unexpected.

So, while the mentoring was very short, the influence was very long.

Anita's book is about profit with principles, where she mentions the day she gave a speech to the business community, which is quite a long time ago now. She told them how she felt business was, and that it was based on greed. People walked out, making comments. I think now we have to make a much bigger change than pussyfooting and tinkering around at the edges of what the real issues are, and Anita understood that well. Mohammed Yunis (a Nobel Peace Prize-winning economist who pioneered the concept of microcredit) says the same in his books, the *Forbes* Index says it, and Davos 2020 said it this year.

3. What was the best advice she gave you, that you would like to share?

Anita said to me, "You are passionate about things, aren't you?" And also, "You have left your job more than once to follow your passion." I remember this so distinctly. My life experience from a child to adulthood has made me realize how unfair life can be, and like Anita said, "Passion is a guide." She also said in her book that instinct told her where to go with that passion, Passion is your guide and instinct will help you to deal with different challenges; this was something that both Anita and I shared. It was perhaps the best advice she gave me, and I share this with young people when I talk to them. You never know where the seeds you plant are going to grow – the ripple effect that you can have.

As you're aware, Anita sold the business to L'Oréal and joined their board, facing a lot of criticism for that. But what she shared with me was that she wanted to be on the board to make a change within this huge organization, to improve their sourcing, their whole business model, and that it would take a while to do. Today, L'Oréal is doing lots towards sustainability. Working within, she caused that ripple effect.

I was working at Thames TV when they lost the franchise, and I joined Carlton TV for their launch and where I eventually met Sir Clive Jones, who became CEO. He has backed everything I have done! We've both been on the board of an amazing project, Youth Culture Television (YCTV), and I am very proud that today lots of people from YCTV have gone on to do lots of wonderful things, including Miranda Wayland, who has been appointed this year as the BBC's Head of Creative Diversity.

Clive sent me to the first CSR conference in Europe, to represent ITV. Now, this is very unusual, because I am in the programme-making department, which you will appreciate is different from CSR. But yet, we made programmes that went into Carlton TV's annual report, as we made all the sustainability, social and environmental programmes. We also worked closely with Business in the Community, to help others improve their Triple Bottom Line. When Carlton TV won the franchise, it agreed to give £500,000 annually to grassroots charities, not from fundraising, but from the company itself. This allowed us to make the films for these organizations that Carlton was supporting across London.

Clive sending me to that CSR conference was a real eye-opener, and we were the only TV broadcasting company at the conference. They kept calling us 'press.' I kept trying to explain that we were there representing Carlton's CSR mission, and then it dawned on me that creative industries need CSR just like any other corporate. The music, fashion and film industries all need to have CSR properly in place.

4. **What do you think Anita would think of Greta Thunberg, the Swedish teenager turned environmental activist?**

My first reaction is that they would be friends and colleagues. It would be a friendship based on equality and a meeting of minds. Anita would have not been condescending about Greta's age. You cannot do all the things that Greta has without treating her as an equal. Anita would have been a supporter and would have wanted to have conversations as equals.

5. **What do you think businesses and organizations could be doing better to support the planet for future generations?**

They have to move drastically. And if you look at my area, which is the creative industries, while we saw Michael Eavis, the creator of Glastonbury, make the festival green in the very early days, there is still a huge amount that we could be doing that is different. The creative industry in this country is one of our biggest growth areas, which can be tweaked to be environmental and have a social impact.

I believe the Triple Bottom Line has to become the Quadruple Bottom Line, and we've been talking about it long enough. The financial, environmental and social performance are of equal value. We can use big data now to look at it, and we can also use the Triple Bottom Line. There is enough evidence to show impact and measurement. It can no longer just be about the shareholders and money. Businesses cannot function like this any more.

We need action today: one, to save the plant, and two, to distribute wealth fairly. Companies can do that

– instead of greed being their motive, it has to be kindness and a revolution for change. They must embrace purpose and social impact. If (UK retailers) John Lewis and Waitrose can pay a dividend to their staff, so can all companies.

While it is a certain class of people who can make those choices, I also think ordinary people deserve companies to give them that choice. It's not just about the wealthy. In India, exporting via Fairtrade is great, but it's geared towards people with a certain income. I am working on a project in Africa at the moment, a continent where it has to be about sharing the world's resources. And, crucially, it is not imposing our western style of business inappropriately, which is a form of colonialism. I don't see it being any different.

6. **China is a country that's been criticized for its sustainability record around the world. Do you think China will change?**

When I speak to students at universities, the majority want to do something good, set up as social entrepreneurs, and only want to work in companies where they feel that they're doing social good. We've had a revolution in this country, and Europe, where a lot of children have grown up knowing about environmental impact. Now, in China, we have an interesting situation. It's a very different political landscape, where we still have analogue thinkers running China, just like we had here. They are not digital natives. In this country, and around the world, thousands of Chinese students have been educated.

I have been following China since they started building cricket stadiums in the Caribbean, then taking all the bauxite, and when they built stadiums in Africa, mining all the minerals, so you could argue that there's a long-term (goal of) domination of the world.

But I suspect, just like in India – with the new generation that has come through, who want to make change – they have an international outlook for positive change and want social good to be part of what they do. My hope is that it's the same for Chinese students, who have seen and enjoyed a different type of education. That they will want their companies they establish to also be more aware of the planet. They don't want to be living their lives with terrible pollution in parts of China.

I hope the digital China, which I know is isolated digitally at the moment, will become a different China. I have a genuine belief that the majority of people in this world do want kindness, that they do want fairness, and do recognize it's a better world for that. I believe that the next generation of young Chinese will be very different. They have studied globally, but I am not saying that they will take back colonial values. It will be their own brand of whatever country they want to shape and have.

I was just amazed how much all of us on the UnLtd (social entrepreneur foundation) trip learned from the young people in India, where many of them where the first generation coming from extreme poverty. But they were all doing something philanthropic with their lives and wanted to give back. I can't imagine that Chinese students would be any different. They are human beings. My hope is my experience. I have not travelled anywhere in the world where people genuinely don't want a better place for people. Young people that I know want to be participating in a world that is fairer, and not one that is exploitative of either ordinary people or the planet.

Chapter 2

WHAT
CUSTOMERS,
EMPLOYEES AND
STAKEHOLDERS
EXPECT

In 2015, a Cone Communications/Ebiquity Global CSR study found that 91% of consumers worldwide expect businesses to operate responsibly to address social and environmental issues.[11] The key findings include:

- 91% of global consumers expect companies to do more than make a profit; to also operate responsibly to address social and environmental issues

- 84% say they seek out responsible products whenever possible

- 90% would boycott a company if they learned of irresponsible or deceptive business practices

Similarly, the annual Nielsen Global Corporate Sustainability Report reveals that 81% of respondents feel strongly that companies should help improve the environment. Research in 2016 by the academics Magda BL Donia, Carol-Ann Tetrault Sirsly and Sigalit Ronen showed that employees didn't respond well if they believed their organization was using CSR to give a false impression of virtue.[12]

Countless studies have demonstrated that the tides are turning, and that organizations need to be careful to engage in CSR for the right reasons. People trust organizations that engage in genuine CSR, but distrust those that engage in greenwashing.

THE GRETA THUNBERG EFFECT

Before COVID-19 we had something called the 'Greta Thunberg Effect,' named after the Swedish teenager whose environmental campaigning has gained international recognition. After Thunberg addressed the 2018 UN Climate Change Conference, student strikes took place every week somewhere in the world. Her stark message on an overheating Earth dominated the news cycle. In 2019, there were coordinated multi-city protests involving over a million students each, and these organized demonstrations continue. Her influence on the world stage was soon dubbed the 'Greta Effect' by *The Guardian* and other leading media.

Growing concern over the climate crisis, aided by the 'Greta Effect' – along with the birth of the global Extinction Rebellion movement, demanding that politics respond to the urgency of the situation – are driving huge increases in individuals and businesses choosing to offset their emissions by investing in carbon-reducing projects in developing countries. This all further positions social responsibility and ethical practices as vital components to business success.

THE CONSUMER

When it comes to social responsibility, consumers are looking for brands to show them – not just tell them – what they're doing. Greenwashing and token CSR initiatives are not enough.

In this digital world, where authenticity is the buzzword of choice, businesses must keep up with growing demands for ethical behaviour and transparency in everything, from employee rights and gender equality to supply chain management. This appetite for ethical products, and the emergence of the vegan consumer, has been driven by social media, which has helped fuel the popularity of the plant-based lifestyle. The hashtag #vegan has more than 87 million posts listed on Instagram.

Sustainability will continue to be a key factor impacting shopping behaviour, where consumers are choosing paper and metal straws over plastic ones, along with organic products, non-meat dietary alternatives and cruelty-free brands. Consumers across all age brackets are banding together to fight climate change and, in response, many companies are going green or making zero-waste, package-free products their value proposition, all in a bid to attract environmentally conscious customers.

Recognizing this change, BP's newly appointed CEO, Bernard Looney, shared a new corporate 'purpose' when he took up the mantle in January 2020. His first post on Instagram was to engage directly with society, especially younger people and those who are critical of the fossil fuel company. "I know a lot of people have views on oil and gas companies and our role in the energy transition," he wrote. "I would like to use this platform to talk openly about that and explain the role BP can play, as I believe we share the same concerns and hopes."

Over time, Looney has since sat down with investors, partners, policymakers, NGOs, academics and the global news media to continue that dialogue.

Other brands are also keenly listening and adapting to changing consumer sentiment. For instance, in 2019 the department store chain Selfridges became the first major UK retailer to remove palm oil from all of its own-brand food products. The company instead is using alternatives derived from rapeseed, soybeans and sunflowers until palm oil can be sourced sustainably.

A statement on Selfridge's website quotes Managing Director Simon Forster saying the following: "We believe that until certified palm oil guarantees zero deforestation, our customers should be given the option to buy palm oil-free products."[13]

This family-owned business has put sustainability at its core to ensure that it's helping create a livable world for future generations. It's doing so to reduce its direct environmental impact, and encouraging its suppliers and customers to do the same.

Another industry that's changing is the fashion world, where the brands that will succeed are the ones reacting constructively to the shift taking shape around them. There's a dawning realization, here as elsewhere, that the old rules don't fit or work any more. The industry now needs to be able to pivot, think digital-first, take an active stance on social issues, and satisfy consumer demands for ultra-transparency and sustainability. Most importantly, the apparel sector recognizes that it needs to have the guts to self-disrupt its own identity in order to win new generations of customers.

In fact, some fashion brands have turned to hackathons – intensive group software development events – to come up with new technology innovations to foster sustainability. Companies such as Kering and LVMH are awarding prizes to developers, students and experts who can help solve supply chain management and overproduction issues. However, without proper resources or metrics in place, hackathons run the risk of becoming 'ideathons,' where topics are discussed but nothing happens. Also, while some fashion brands behave responsibly, so-called 'fast fashion' brands have been exposed for who and what they are, employing production practices that destroy the planet and exploit human labour. These brands are continuously marketing to ensure that you're constantly shopping for the latest trends. They're swiftly killing the planet and co-opting your ethics, and the best bit from their perspective is you don't even realize it.

Something else to think about is diversity, inclusion and belonging, which have become increasingly important to the customers you serve. It's especially important when they or someone in their circle are a part of a diversity group. This is being driven by the recent black deaths at the hands of police in America, which has seen increasingly passionate protests as part of the BLM Movement. This has inspired a global conversation about racial injustice. As a result, consumers are now looking to their favourite brands for action against systemic racism. Some companies, such as Glossier and Nike, have responded by donating millions to organizations fighting racial injustice, Others have posted messages of solidarity on Instagram. Yet, one of the biggest challenges brands face in producing effective inclusive marketing – particularly for diverse audiences – is a lack of cultural intelligence regarding the audience they're trying to cater to.

One of the main things you can do to increase your, and your employees', understanding of your diverse customer groups is hire diverse core and extended teams. Someone who has effectively done this is Edward Enniful, who became the editor-in-chief of *British Vogue* in 2017. He addressed the diversity debate with his first issue of the magazine, putting mixed-race model and feminist activist Adwoa Aboah on the cover. Since then, he has continued to shake things up and push for positive change.

In June 2020, via the online *Hope Vogue* platform, Enninful said: "Celebrating real people is something that has always been intrinsic to the identity of *British Vogue*, but I have been even more inspired in recent weeks. We've learnt lessons for the future, too: for me, the conversation moving forward will be even more laser-focussed on sustainability and ecological issues. In terms of our fashion shoots, they will be more concise, and everything will be super edited. If you have a great idea, you just need one wonderful look to make it work. It goes without saying, too, that with everything that is happening in the world right now, diversity continues to be a driving principle."[14]

However, at the same time, across the pond, there were big diversity issues exploding at *Bon Appétit*. The glossy food magazine is part of the Condé Nast group, a global media company that produces an array of titles such as *GQ, The New Yorker, Vanity Fair, Wired* and *Vogue*. Adam Rapoport, *Bon Appétit's* editor-in-chief, came under fire over allegations that Condé Nast only paid white editors for video appearances. Rapoport was then forced to resign when an old photo of him in an offensive costume surfaced on social media. The image underscored the problems at the magazine, including a workplace culture of racial insensitivity.

This kind of behaviour is no longer tolerated, and when it rears its head, it doesn't go away until decisive action is taken.

If you're just getting started marketing to a niche customer group – particularly one that you aren't personally a part of – be sure to create a diverse, inclusive team with more than one member of that customer group. This should include your brand team, agency partners, consultants, and even your market research team.

The more you surround yourself with people who have deep knowledge of the customers you want to reach, the easier it will be to effectively combine that with experiences, ideas and points of view from others on the team and create the right material – relevant content that truly connects. Good examples of businesses getting it right are beauty brands Fenty Beauty and Glossier (again) who understand the value of staying culturally relevant. It's becoming increasingly important for people to feel that brands reflect them as a consumer. It's not enough to show a lineup of exclusively white, blonde, impossibly slim women any more.

EXPECTATIONS OF THE NEW WORKFORCE

Today, 30% of workers are millennials, with baby boomers reaching retirement and the 22-38-year-old set stepping in. According to *Brookings Data Now*, by 2025 some 75% of the workforce will be made up of millennials.[15] Therefore, businesses that want to stay competitive in the hiring market, and recruit the best talent, need to understand that millennials are not looking for the same things from their employers that the boomers wanted.

Baby boomers sought workplaces that offered stability and high pay. Millennials have different priorities and want different things. They have high expectations for businesses when it comes to social purpose and accountability, and they want to work for companies that uphold these values. This means your company will have to evolve and innovate in order to stay relevant, attract quality employees and retain top performers in the new millennial marketplace.

People are motivated and more willing to go the extra mile to make the company successful when there's a higher good associated with it – it's no longer about just being a job. Work becomes meaningful and this makes us more competitive.

These are the six primary ways that CSR programmes help employee relations. A socially responsible company:

1. **Inspires Better Citizenship Behaviours And Improved Employee Relationships.** If employees think their employer is doing the right thing, they're more likely to do the right thing themselves. When organizations implement best practices in CSR, employees are more likely to engage in cooperative behaviours with their co-workers and the organization, such as going out of their way to help a teammate. It also promotes closer, higher-quality relationships between employees.

2. **Fosters Better Employee Affinity With The Business.** When employees feel that their organization is socially responsible, they experience a greater sense of identitfying with the business/brand. These days, social responsibility can be more important than financial success in determining how much employees identify with their workplace.

3. **Increases Retention And Organizational Commitment.** Feeling positive about their organization's CSR initiative has been shown to increase employees' intention to stay with the company, and their overall commitment to the organization. Commitment includes a huge range of positive attitudes, including

how much employees like their organization, make personal sacrifices for it, and see their own future and success tied to its success.

4. Attracts Talent. Along with increasing current employees' commitment, CSR can also make firms look more attractive to applicants and prospective employees. At a time when millennials want to work for 'high impact' organizations, engaging in CSR may help companies attract top talent in an ever-more-competitive marketplace.

5. Encourages Better Employee Engagement And Performance. Employees have shown to be more engaged and to perform better when they feel good about their company's CSR involvement. By making them aware of the company's efforts to give back, and celebrating these efforts, you can help employees become more actively engaged with their work... and actually do better at it.

6. Increases Creativity. CSR can increase employees' creative involvement, including generating new ideas and engaging in creative problem solving. When companies express their values and passions through CSR, employees may be inspired to develop new and better ways to do their work.

SINCE COVID-19

All of the above has been overshadowed by the global pandemic, and recent international consumer surveys show that uncertainty and fear are driving sentiment and behaviour. The virus has forcefully disrupted life for billions of people worldwide, and uncertainty has become a constant for individuals, businesses and organizations of all types.

The digital marketing company Astound Commerce conducted surveys of consumers in the US, Canada, Europe and the Middle East in early March 2020, asking about concerns, changes in daily life and overall outlook on what the future holds. It found that 75% of respondents had fears about the coronavirus outbreak, with the highest fear level in the Middle East (96%), and the lowest in Europe and the US (68% and 69%, respectively).[16]

Large numbers of respondents indicated that they'd been impacted by the virus in terms of the shopping experience. Almost half, across all geographies, reported out-of-stock product issues. In the US, 38% of consumers claimed to have encountered product shortages.

A weekly consumer survey by the Boston Consulting Group had similar findings. And a snapshot from other early-March 2020 research in the US revealed fear as a driver, impacting consumer behaviour in everything from travel, everyday activities and work practices to government interventions. Data showed that 46% of Americans surveyed believed 'the world is in serious danger,' and 56% believed there would be a recession. A staggering 65% said they believed the 'worst impacts are ahead.'[17]

What these new surveys show, along with the 'Greta Effect,' is that businesses need to engage with their next generation of consumers, who are demanding changes in the way goods are produced and the way companies treat the planet. Consumers around the world are making adjustments in their shopping habits.

CHALLENGING TIMES ARE ALSO FERTILE GROUND FOR CHANGE

With growing resource volatility, species extinction and concerns around climate change and global warming, we can see that the world we live in is more aware than ever of the need to go down a more sustainable path.

However, businesses often ignore CSR values and are reluctant to place sustainability where it should be: at the core of their strategies and operations. This is largely because there's still a general misperception that the cost of sustainability outweighs the benefits. Yet, we can see that consumers are willing to pay for products and services that are greener and better for the planet. Sadly, many businesses are stuck in the mindset of optimizing short-term financial performance while overlooking market drivers and the potential for long-term success.

The truth is, economic gain and value creation for shareholders should not have to come at the expense of other stakeholders. There's mounting evidence to support the notion that sustainability and profits do not have to be mutually exclusive.

Also, remember that all businesses – big or small, new or established – need to think about how reflective their workforce is of the diversity within our societies. As businesses, we can no longer be blind or ignorant. Especially now, in these challenging economic times brought about by the pandemic, using the talents of the whole workforce is more important than ever. At the same time, fostering an inclusive working environment can bring business benefits and provide a market advantage in economically straightened times. The current situation also provides fertile ground for change-makers to emerge.

IN CONVERSATION...
WITH JAMES QUINN

In April 2020 I spoke to James Quinn, CEO of UK-based Faradion, the world leader in non-aqueous sodium-ion cell technology. This is the most promising alternative to lithium-ion batteries, which involve exploitative production processes and can emit toxic gasses, catch fire and explode. James is a proven technology products executive, with over 25 years' experience in systems and services, including product development in leading-edge technologies, global supply chain management, manufacturing, distribution and licensing.

The world needs more CEOs like James, who possess a real global outlook and strong sustainable values, to help create the change that we and the planet so desperately need.

1. **Do you think businesses in general need to become more sustainable with their models and products?**
From my side, absolutely, especially if we look back at the environment when the world was struck by the virus. It was clear the impact humans have had on the environment and we could see what was possible. Suddenly, there were people in parts of the north of India who could see the Himalayas for

the first time in decades. Since then, things have gone back to normal, planes are flying again, people are driving and the pollution levels have increased, but I think the pandemic has left a mark on us. We can't forget. We need to keep the pressure on, and for governments, companies, consumers and employees across the board to look for more sustainable environmental solutions.

There are a lot of companies that have been around for a long time in the battery industry, where many lithium-ion batteries have cobalt in them, and 25% of cobalt is informally mined, which basically means child labour. We've seen some of the villages in the Congo suing companies such as Apple, Google and others for the violations of human and environmental rights over cobalt. As a result, companies are putting more CSR emphasis at the forefront of their operations with regards to cobalt, which is a knee jerk reaction for their business. I believe in a proactive approach and finding more sustainable technology.

2. **Do you think companies are doing enough to incorporate CSR into their business strategies, for their employees and their customers?**
Well, I like the title of your book, because CSR is not PR. I think many companies treat CSR like PR, where they put CSR on their website, or say they are using reusable energy or whatever, but in my view it's all very 'PRish' and CSR is not deep or ingrained as a core value of the company. It's too easy to put the PR stamp on things. Hopefully this is changing, and employees and consumers will hold companies

to a higher standard than purely a marketing logo or initiative.

We see a lot of the younger generation more focused on the environment and I think it's forcing us to think differently – particularly my generation, who were from a more disposable society. Our children are taking a more active role and creating change. They're getting us to rethink our approach and holding us accountable. I also think consumers and employees hold us accountable, and they should. I think it's very important to businesses to look to that.

3. Do you think there is going to be demand for more sodium-ion technology globally?

During the pandemic, we issued a press release (in April 2020, announcing an Australian battery contract) and I could not believe the attention it received and the response we had to the sodium-ion technology. It went off the scale for us, where we had all kinds of traction from Australia, India and the US. People were, and still are, very interested.

If you look at the battery/energy storage business, which is our business, it's really controlled by China, and energy is such a key thing. If we take a look at India, it's the largest importer of oil in the world, and if you look at the 30 most polluted cities in the world, 22 of them are in India. It's a huge problem for India. Prime Minister Modi has been talking about reducing dependency on oil, but it has increased significantly since he has been in office. The reason is because if you want to go towards renewable energy, and get away from dependence on fossil fuels and oil, you find yourself stuck between the Middle East or China.

China controls nearly 80% of the manufacturing capacity for lithium-ion technology. They control the material supply chain, and the materials make up 75–80% of the cell cost. China has the largest refinement of cobalt capabilities, and 65% of the world's graphite supply, which is used in lithium-ion batteries. China has 30 times more lithium reserves, as compared to the US. Therefore, if you want to produce lithium-ion batteries in India, you are still dependent on China.

Countries now have a choice, and I think it's why there's been so much interest in our sodium-ion technology – not just from India, but from Australia, the US and Europe. These regions have the opportunity to gain energy security. This means that you can produce sodium-ion batteries outside of China, and more importantly, source the materials locally. They have the potential for an indigenous, integrated, vertical supply chain.

For India, it's a big opportunity to leap-frog to next-generation technology, where it can source locally, giving them the option of having sustainable energy. This is not just for India, but for Australia, too, and we're working with partners there who previously owned lithium mines. Australia has one of the largest deposits of lithium in the world, and China has a lot of investments here. Our partners sold these lithium mines and have gone all in for sodium. Sodium (salt) is the sixth most abundant element on the Earth, and it's everywhere: in the oceans, in the earth. It really is an unlimited resource.

In our technology there's no cobalt, no lithium, no graphite and no copper. For example, it costs $15,000 a tonne to mine lithium, as opposed to $150 a tonne to harvest sodium. Economically, it makes sense. It gives a country national and environmental security.

4. **Why has Faradion focused on India? Is it going to be a leader in next-gen battery technology?**
Our batteries give India huge potential to reduce its dependence on other countries and cut its pollution. We're developing a partnership in India to manufacture sodium-ion batteries. It makes sense on so many levels to look at India, which is dealing with its own challenges from pollution, having the second biggest population in the world and being oil dependent. Therefore, it has a lot of opportunity to develop a new 'next generation.'

Lithium-ion batteries have been out for the last 30 years, and we need to bring in new technology. But the technology has to be more sustainable, environmentally friendly, cleaner, lower-cost, with great performance. I think India is right for these factors.

Faradion has a patent on 'zero volt' capability for safety and transportation. This means our sodium-ion batteries are safer and resistant to abuse from overcharging or undercharging. Our sodium-ion batteries can be shipped, installed and have maintenance performed at zero volts. This is very important in countries which do not have a mature charging infrastructure. There is high risk for mistreatment of lithium-ion batteries when people recharge them at uncertified roadside shops or in their homes, which may cause a fire. Safety, whether it is environmental or the safety of human lives, is a top priority for Faradion.

5. **The world is still struggling to emerge from the COVID-19 pandemic. Do you think it's had a significant impact on how the global energy sector operates?**
The pandemic has shown us that we need security in food and energy. If we look at the supply chain for a moment, when China suddenly shut down we couldn't get air conditioning units, batteries, wedding dresses – China controls so many main supply chains in the world. I think one of the things the pandemic has shown us, particularly in countries like India, is that the world has become so dependent on a single region, in this case China, who may not share the same values on sustainability or be as environmentally conscious as other countries.

This is why I think the supply chains should be re-examined. As we get back to normal, there are new opportunities for sustainability, which can look at the environmental impact of supply chains.

6. **Faradion is collaborating with some interesting partners, such as the University of Warwick and the University of Oxford. Can you share how you are partnering?**
We work with a variety of universities and we do different things with all our university partners, as each place has different areas of expertise and strengths. For example, at the University of Sheffield they have a lot of testing capability. We work with

partners to qualify the technology. We develop the technology on our own – it's our intellectual property – and then work with partners like Warwick, Oxford, etc., to produce more prototypes. Then we work with qualified, licensed partners to scale the technology, and Faradion sells the product to the customer, whether it's for telecommunications or electric vehicles.

We partner carefully. It's based on capabilities and the need to meet our green criteria, where organizations are not just dumping their chemical waste. Plus, our investors would expect that from us.

7. As a CEO in business, are you concerned about the future of our planet?

Oh, yes. Especially now, when I see what harm we have done, I am also worried for our children's future. It sounds really clichéd, and there's that expression, 'We didn't inherit the earth; we're watching it for our children.' Well, I think there's definitely truth to that, and I am concerned.

It almost hurts me to see what we have done to the earth. When you look at the virus, one of the good things to have come from it was that it woke people up to what is possible.

We all saw that, in just that short period, when most of the world had been in lockdown, there was an improvement in our atmosphere. It started in China, and when China shut down, the satellite pictures showed clean, clear skies for the first time in years. Scientific data showed that the crisis temporarily cut CO_2 emissions in China by 25%. Other data suggested the pandemic shutdown caused global emissions to reduce in the region of 2,000m tonnes of CO2. As a result, we have seen what's possible.

We regularly receive enquiries from companies with electric airline initiatives, who are looking at what can be done. And it's not just airlines, but also for drones, helicopters – all types of aviation can use electric batteries.

We had a company come to us for flying cars, which, while really cool, we're still a business and there's probably not a lot of volume for us. We have to pick the right markets, where we can have a broader impact and have enough volume to bring down the cost.

Otherwise, the technology works out more expensive, and will make it difficult for people to make that transition. We have to find a way to bridge that gap. It's why we try to work with large-scale industrialization partners that can help us commercialize our technology – do it in the volumes that can bring the cost down, that can make it accessible for people.

We at Faradion are continually looking to improve our sustainability impact and want to keep making a difference, driving change forward!

IN CONVERSATION
WITH AISHA RAHEEM

This conversation takes us to Nigeria, to meet entrepreneur Aisha Raheem, founder of Farmz2U, a business that uses technology to empower farmers. I spoke to Aisha in May 2020.

Farmz2U is working to increase food sustainability and security by helping farmers adopt sustainable farming methods with increased access to market. Aisha and her team recognize that, with 25% of the global population predicted to reside in Africa by 2050, the continent must expand its agricultural production capacity to ensure food sustainability. The Sub-Saharan African region has the resources necessary to grow its agricultural industry, but needs help.

Aisha was the perfect person to speak with in terms of understanding the challenges of setting up CSR-led businesses and gaining a general overview of how things work in her region.

1. **What have been the business challenges for Farmz2U since you launched in Nigeria?**

It has been a mix of challenges. One of the main ones is the speed of being able to set up a business here is slow. For example, in the UK, I set up my business in half an hour, while here in Nigeria – where there are numerous paper documents to sign and physical business sites to visit – it has taken me about six months. Another challenge has been the lack of infrastructure, where the business processes are not straightforward. Again, citing the UK as an example, there you have different regulatory bodies, governing certain industries, that do not exist here. The third challenge is access to capital, as there isn't a lot of financial support or as many grant schemes as we find in advanced economies. That said, at Farmz2U we've been able to access grant schemes, to be able to afford office space. Also, local investors have a different outlook and are probably not as sophisticated, as they want to invest in familiar sectors such as real estate, rather than anything that might be different.

However, while these have been challenges, I also see them as opportunities. It means that there's less red tape to deal with and it's easier to start a business than in advanced countries, because the regulator and government are behind you. As a result, start-ups are leading the way here and the fintech sector has grown exponentially; companies in Nigeria have really mushroomed in the last three to five years. Now, the government is introducing regulation to try to control how these businesses are operating.

2. How is CSR interpreted in Nigeria by the business world? And, how do you think it is perceived across Africa?
Again, it's a mix. I've been able to travel to other African countries, and from what I have seen CSR is different in other African nations. In places like Uganda, Tanzania and Rwanda, single-use plastic is banned. In these places, there are public and private efforts to ensure that when it comes to zero plastic waste, it is nil – reduced to the bare minimum. In Nigeria it's the total opposite, where there's total disregard for plastic waste. For example, when I go to the shopping mall I take my own shopping bags, and if I run out of

bags I ask the traders not to pack my shopping in lots of separate plastic bags.

Also, in the conversations I have with my social circles in Nigeria about the environmental impact of single-plastic waste and the flaring of gas by oil companies (Nigeria is the largest oil producer in Africa, holding the largest natural gas reserves on the continent), people say, 'That's a First World problem.' That's because most people are more concerned about their next meal and don't really care about ethical practices. Yet, when it rains, the plastic bags and other waste clog the drains, and then water overflows and there's flooding. Again, flared gas could be used as an alternative source of energy. There isn't a full understanding here about CSR or sustainability. What we need is more education from the government. In countries like Uganda, Rwanda and Tanzania, they were able to introduce policy, because they educated people about reducing plastic waste and the benefits, which has had a direct impact on the cities in these places, where cleanliness has improved. In Nigeria, there are no incentives for business or the end user to care about these things. Neither is there anyone holding businesses accountable to put good practices in place.

3. Is there demand from consumers here for businesses to be ethically led?
Increasingly, I am seeing an interest in ethically-led businesses. However, I don't think there's real demand as yet and, if there is demand, it's from a very small group of consumers. People here don't necessarily care where their food is coming from,

or the conditions of who made their food. For instance, we have food hawkers, who sell food on the roads, where you can also buy the same or similar item of food in the supermarket for $3, but people will bargain with the street trader, trying to buy it for 50 cents. So, the consumer behaviour here is not driven by quality or sustainability, with little care about the street hawkers, who are most likely to be people from poorer communities. Therefore, the challenges are different here.

Also, when you think about ethics, the banks make a lot of money in Nigeria; some yearly growth figures are in triple figures. Yet, when you look at the activities of the banks, you wonder what are they actually doing for communities here? How are they giving back when they have ridiculous profit margins?

You can say the same about the telecommunications industry, too. There are very few companies that have CSR initiatives – there's DStv, which is part of MultiChoice from South Africa; MTN; Coca-Cola, which is a global company. But if you look at their CSR activities locally, as opposed to elsewhere, I think they could be doing more.

But then, the demand for ethical and sustainable businesses is not high enough. If consumers and the public wanted it, the government would be clamping down on these companies, making them invest more in CSR initiatives here. I think it will come, in more established countries, such as the UK. It only introduced the 5p plastic bag fee in supermarkets about five years ago, and now this 'conscious consumer' thinking has grown and influenced other shopping behaviours.

4. Is there any government support for CSR-led businesses there?

Not that I have seen. I might be wrong. If it's not being demanded by established businesses here, which would be the starting point in my view, then it won't be implemented by government and is not high enough on the government agenda.

5. What business advice would you give start-ups in this region who have a focus on sustainability?

While I see there's no demand for CSR in the country, I still think building businesses with CSR values and mindset is a wise thing to do. Especially because businesses are global, and you will want to be perceived as a business that is cognizant and aware of the environmental changes that are happening, and affecting us all. This is evident in the type of start-ups that are emerging here, where there are lots of recycling companies and sustainable building materials. Businesses in the African region should remember that sustainability in the west was not a cool topic in the beginning and, over time, ethical and sustainable businesses have grown and become popular.

My other advice is to have a clear business purpose, and the money will come eventually. Everything will flow from your purpose. You might incur up-front costs, but there's evidence that there are strong business benefits in the long term.

We are running out of time with the earth's resources, and we can't wait for governments to catch up. We need to be proactive in positioning ourselves to create the businesses that have the solutions. We also need to educate the government and the people.

6. **Do you think there's a rise of 'ethical entrepreneurs' emerging in Africa?**

Yes, definitely! There's been a rise in fintech and health tech start-ups, such as 54gene, which aims to improve drug discovery by researching the genetically-diverse African population. There's a rise in start-ups trying to solve the ethical issues here – for Africans, by Africans.

There is also work being done by some emerging companies who are creating more transparency to help erode the corruption. There is a rise, and in terms of driving growth, small- and medium-sized enterprises are the bedrock of any country's growth. Ethical entrepreneurs are the ones driving the movement, those who are able to build in a sustainable way, working towards a better economy.

7. **What is it like being a female entrepreneur in Nigeria?**

I am trying to think, is it much different from being a female entrepreneur in London, where I also ran a business? I think not. It's fun and crazy at the same time, where I get to meet amazing people on my journey, and that's what any entrepreneur will experience. A female entrepreneur anywhere in the world will probably have the same experience, where her skills may be questioned, and her ability to run a business. But I have not experienced that being here. I've been respected, and been able to successfully build my team of five and attract talent.

I also think that the global economy recognizes that women play a very important role when it comes to business. And on the African continent,

Rwanda has the most diverse female cabinet, and its economy is thriving. That says something. I think Africa might be ahead of the curve with female inclusion! But then, there's still that patriarchal concept here, where the woman is meant to be a wife, meant to be at home and have children. There's still that thinking and mindset, but I do think we're moving away from that. And when you look at businesses that are thriving, lots of them are being led by women.

Chapter 3

INDIA

LEADING THE WAY WITH CSR LAW

India is a country full of diversity and contradictions.

While per-capita greenhouse gas emissions are among the lowest in the world, India is the third-biggest generator of these climate-altering gasses. It may be the third-largest economy in the world, but the country also has the greatest number of people living below the international poverty line.

Despite of these challenges, India is a conscious, progressive aspirant. In April 2014, it became the first country in the world to make CSR mandatory, following an amendment to the Companies Act, its business incorporation law. Since then, other countries have followed suit, including China and Indonesia.

Through this law, businesses there can invest their profits in areas such as education, poverty relief, gender equality and hunger remediation, as part of their CSR compliance. All businesses, nationals and multinationals, with annual revenues of more than ₹10 billion (£105 million) must give 2% of their net profit to charity. The Indian government believes the law will release much-needed funds for social development, and the general consensus has been that it's working. The legislative change has made corporate India wake up to its wider social responsibilities, and the domestic press has reported positively on its impact.

Data shows that, since 2014, CSR spending by corporate India has increased significantly: in 2018, companies spent 47% more than in 2014–2015, contributing US $1 billion to CSR initiatives. Listed companies in India spent US $1.4 billion on various programmes, ranging from education, skill development, social welfare and healthcare to environment conservation.[18] The Prime Minister's Relief Fund saw an increase of 139% in CSR contribution in its launch year, 2019.

The education sector received the most funding (38% of the total) followed by hunger, poverty and healthcare (25%), environmental sustainability (12%) and rural development (11%). Meanwhile, projects involving technology incubators, sports, armed forces and reducing inequalities saw almost negligible spends. Industry research estimates see CSR compliance improving, into the range of 97–98% in 2020.

Having lived in India, I know that sustainability has always been a core component of the national culture. Indian philosophy and values have underscored a sustainable way of life. This is a country with one of the least wasteful economies, frequently acknowledged for its efforts to mitigate climate change and achieve environmental sustainability. This has been the result of energy-efficiency policy measures and international dialogue, especially after India emerged as a key player in shaping the 2016 Paris Agreement, part of the UN Framework Convention on Climate Change.

India is a nation steeped in spirituality and yogic principles, where yoga and Ayurveda are among the hallmarks of holistic Indian living. Yoga, which is a Sanskrit word, is an ancient physical, mental and spiritual practice that originated in India. It means 'to join' or 'to unite,' symbolizing the union of body and consciousness. Today, yoga is practiced in various forms around the world, and it continues to grow in popularity. It is also one of India's best exports, and now plays an important role in the global sustainability agenda.

Recognizing its universal appeal, the UN in 2014 declared 21 June 'International Day of Yoga' – an annual opportunity to raise global awareness of the many benefits of practicing yoga. Indian Prime Minister Narendra Modi proposed the idea to the UN, and it was endorsed by a record 175 member states. At that time, Modi said, "Yoga is not just about exercise; it is a way to discover the sense of oneness with yourself, the world and nature."[19]

This was a smart move by India because, by promoting yoga, it has become recognized as the country of its origin, and a source of natural wellbeing and 'protector of the environment.'

This brand positioning cleverly builds on India's soft power, which at the same time attracts investment. India has learned through experience the importance of owning its cultural brands. For instance, 20 years ago the Texas company RiceTec tried to trademark Basmati Rice, a variety developed by Indian farmers over hundreds of years and coveted for its fragrant taste and long, delicate grains. The Indian government challenged the move, marking the first time a developing country opposed a US company trying to patent – and control the production of – a staple food crop. The Indian government prevailed in the case, and RiceTec went to sell a variety called Texmati, a hybrid of Basmati and American long-grain rice, in the North American market.

Sustainable and environmentally friendly practices continue to be part of the Indian lifestyle and culture. The country has a culture of thriftiness, reuse and hand-me-downs, and has always had a tradition of recycling through its traditional 'raddi-wallahs,' where items with no value, such as old newspapers, books and utensils, can be easily sold off to a scrap dealer to be reused or recycled.

However, India comprises a vast and complex region, with extreme poverty and wealth, and a deep split between urban and rural populations. That is why CSR is one of the best ways to create transformation across the sub-continent. Yet, many Indian business leaders are focused mainly on regulatory compliance, not core sustainability. The majority of CEOs have said that they face no pressure from investors to move the needle on sustainability. Therefore, if India wants to promote corporate sustainability, pressure will need to increase – and come from all angles – to compel quick and meaningful progress. The most effective drivers are government regulations and standards, subsidies and incentives, and public investment in green technologies.

IN CONVERSATION... WITH NANDHIJI

In September 2020, it was my privilege to speak with Nandhiji for this book. Nandhiji is a visionary yogi, humanitarian and author who splits his time between the US and India. His teachings are of the seldom-revealed source of yogic wisdom of the Siddha Sages, the liberated mystics of South India, and gives us a 'yogic perspective.' He shared some compelling insights.

1. **What role does Yoga play with regard to sustainability? Is there a relationship between the two?**

Yoga practice has been proven to create more awareness and mindfulness amongst its practitioners. The goal of yoga is to enhance and expand consciousness, and one of the attributes of consciousness is to look at humanity and the planet as a whole. Yoga is also about unity. Therefore, it is natural for yoga practitioners to be sensitive to global warming and the current perils that affect us all as humans.

Looking at the growing global yoga community, what is clear is the change occurring, taking the example of eating habits, where now most yoga practitioners are moving from a non-vegetarian to a vegetarian or vegan diet. This shift in eating habits is partially due to mindfulness and understanding the principle of 'ahimsa,' which means non-harming, non-violence and compassion towards all other living beings. This includes, for some, a conscious effort to assist with the sustainability of our planet Earth, by giving up meat and, for some yogis, better health choices.

There is a strong relationship between yoga and sustainability. The practice of yoga promises the evolution of an optimal mind that encourages sustainability, from a change in eating habits to a more intelligent way of life, such as in the use of renewables.

2. What could we all be doing as a humanity to help the planet?

Mahatma Gandhiji said, "Be the change you wish to see in the world." And as yogic wisdom, this saying works well with the '100th Monkey Theory,' a hypothetical phenomenon where a new behaviour or idea is said to spread rapidly, by an unexplained means, from one group to other related groups, once a critical number of members of one group exhibit the new behaviour or acknowledge the new idea. With yoga, meditation, tai chi and all other means that encourage us to go within to seek our own truth, we wake up to being a better human, who is more sensitive to others, to all life and for planet Earth.

So, the first action for us to do is to start our own practice of going inwards. Yoga is a good instrument that helps us on this journey to expand consciousness.

3. What role does India have in the world with regard to sustainability? Has India lost her way?

From the Greek philosopher Aristotle, who influenced Alexander the Great's ambition to go all the way to India, to Fa Hien & Huan Tsuan, the monks of China, India has always been the land of wisdom. It is a country that has culturally dominated most of the Far East and Middle-East Asia, not through expansionism or aggression, but through trade and the philosophy of yoga.

India has been built on the bedrock of a civilization that questioned dogma, which has progressed through greater thoughts and sustained seekers of truth. It has always honoured all religious paths. It was this consciousness that supported India as a superpower in the economic sense for thousands of years. In today's world, the International Yoga Day presented by India to the globe reaffirms the ancient wealth of India with consciousness. Yoga is a potent medicine for the health and vitality of our body and mind. It is an inner journey that does not force religion, beliefs or dogma of any kind on the practitioner. Instead, it generously gifts one with both a mind that is more optimal and with more vigorous health.

I find that monotheist religions are fearful of yoga, because we yoga practitioners are prone to raise questions about religion, lifestyle, eating habits and moral values.

Sadly, yes, India did lose her way after imperial colonialism, where there was purging of its yoga science for Western values in all walks of life. India is female, and in Hindi we say 'Bhārat Mata,' which is from Sanskrit. In English it means 'Mother India,' and it's the national personification of India as a mother goddess who is usually depicted as a woman clad in a saffron sari, holding the Indian national flag, and sometimes is accompanied by a lion.

It has only been in the last six years of India's recent history that it is once again being recognized for its ancient wealth of yoga, holistic health, the greater upkeep and care of natural resources, forests, wildlife and pollution controls.

4. What is the mission and desired result of your Declaration of Consciousness Movement?

Consciousness is the only real, true, meaningful content in every religion, and the Declaration of Consciousness Movement was born with the goal for us as people of the Earth to come together in consciousness as one humanity.

There are nine aspects of the movement: non-violence, women's equality, children's welfare, respecting elders, freedom of thought, equality, righteousness, the upkeep of the planet and unity amongst us all, as one humanity, honouring all paths of consciousness. These are inherent and intrinsic rights of every human, across nations.

The Declaration of Consciousness Movement wants to reach everyone through different activities – from enterprise to entertainment, to media services and information – because when there is consciousness, there is an optimal mind. Abundance, goodness and collective intelligence become ultimate solutions.

One of the principles of the movement is sustainability, as we all know that every life form on our planet depends on us humans to make conscious environmental decisions, which will shape our global climate and physical plane. Without this mindfulness, life as we know it cannot be sustained.

We are also developing our Consciousness Technology Platform that offers conscious content of self-empowerment, movies and documentaries, organizations, information, media, commerce and services, which are all destined to enlighten our awareness. This includes providing you with the ability to nominate and suggest content that inspires you. Our online platform aim is to empower everyone to contribute, share, market and monetize their creative talents and gifts to the world.

5. **What wisdom would you like to leave us with, to inspire us to do better?**
Buddha was asked whether he was God. He replied, saying he was 'awake.' The wisdom of being awake means not only being a happier person, but also being able to use our mind with greater efficiency, effectiveness and ability. When we are all able to fulfil our own potential, we arise as one humanity! Be awake.

THE RISE OF INDIA'S SOCIAL ENTREPRENEURS

In the past decade, India has witnessed considerable growth in its social enterprise activity. The number and quality of innovative ideas and business plans has improved due to growing awareness, support, and quality training and workshops available for social entrepreneurs and social enterprise leaders. The social enterprise ecosystem has evolved with support organizations providing direct, indirect, financial and advisory assistance to social enterprises.

Social impact and entrepreneurship are deeply rooted in the Indian ethos. Cooperative and community-owned business models like Amul and Fabindia have existed here since the 1950s, and Ashoka, the global social entrepreneur support organization, introduced the term 'social entrepreneur' in 1981.

There are 24 associations in the country working to influence predominantly small- and medium-sized enterprises, while also supporting social enterprises. Industry associations are fostering growth in the social enterprise space by providing accreditation, enabling access to corporate donors, providing networking opportunities with peer entrepreneurs, conducting seminars and discussions, running grand challenges and funding awards, and producing knowledge products. Prominent industry associations include the Federation of Indian Chambers of Commerce, Associated Chambers of Commerce and Industry of India, the Confederation of Indian Industry, the National Association of Software and Service Companies, and the Indian Impact Investors Council.

Social innovators in India have pioneered sustainable approaches and inclusive business models, and show that models of stakeholder capitalism can indeed work.

CSR-LED COMPANIES IN INDIA

There are many good examples of leading Indian companies that consider social and environmental issues to be as important to their business as financial growth. Here are a few examples:

- **The Green Hotel.** The Chittaranjan Palace in Mysore has been lovingly restored using traditional Indian crafts, providing employment for traditional craftsmen, many of them national award winners.

The Charities Advisory Trust, a UK group, has set the hotel up as a model of sustainable tourism, with all profits distributed to charitable and environmental projects in India. It incorporates energy-saving features, including solar panels and recycled water for the garden. By finding an economic use for the palace and its historic garden, it has been saved it from demolition and redevelopment of the site. An added and wonderful feature is that the hotel's coffee shop, The Malgudi, is run by women – perhaps the first of its kind in the country.

- **Dabur India Ltd.** This is one of the world's largest Ayurvedic and natural health care companies, built on a legacy of over 135 years. The story of Dabur began with the visionary Dr SK Burman, a Bengali physician who wanted to provide effective and affordable treatments for people in remote villages. He started preparing natural cures for the killer diseases of those days, like cholera, malaria and the plague. As news of his treatments spread, he came to be known as the trusted '*daktar*,' or doctor. In 1884, Burman set up Dabur to produce and dispense Ayurvedic medicines to people who had no access to proper treatment. His commitment and passion grew the company from a fledgling medicine mixer in a small Calcutta house to a trusted household name, known for reliability. Dabur's CSR policy is inspired by a question posed by Burman: "What is that life worth which cannot bring comfort to others?" In pursuing its business strategy of introducing products that give consumers health and wellness, Dabur continues to generate an attractive return for shareholders while minimizing its environmental impact and lending a helping hand to the community.

- **Tata Group.** This values-driven organization directs the business operations and growth of the sprawling, global Tata conglomerate. Jamsetji Nusserwanji Tata, who was born into a family of Parsi priests, broke with tradition when he started his own trading firm in 1868, at just 29. His vision inspired the steel, power and hospitality industries in India to build up with experimental new ideas in technology and worker welfare measures, and also set the foundation for scientific education in India. His efforts propelled the country into the league of industrialized nations, but he was also known for his philanthropy. Today, Tata is a global brand that carries out a variety of CSR projects in India, which are community-led and focused on poverty alleviation, women's empowerment, rural community development and other social welfare programmes. The Tata Code of Conduct is the ethical road map for all employees and companies, providing the guidelines by which the group conducts its business.

- **ITC Group.** This conglomerate, with business interests across the hotel, consumer goods, agriculture, IT and packaging sectors, is focused on creating sustainable livelihood and environment protection programmes. ITC's 'Nation First: Sab Saath Badhein' philosophy underlines its core belief in building a globally competitive and profitable Indian enterprise, while championing societal values and serving larger national priorities. It has an excellent global record in sustainability, and has been carbon-positive, water-positive and solid waste recycling-positive for over a decade. The company has generated sustainable livelihood opportunities for some six million people through its activities. Its e-Choupal programme connects rural farmers through the internet for procurement of agriculture products. It covers 40,000 villages and supports over four million farmers; its social and farm forestry programme assists farmers in converting wasteland to pulpwood plantations. Meanwhile, its social empowerment programmes for micro-enterprises and loans have created sustainable livelihoods for over 40,000 rural women. Nearly 41% of the total energy consumed at ITC is from renewable sources, and its luxury hotels have the unique distinction of being LEED Platinum certified.

IN CONVERSATION...
WITH DR PIYUSH MEHTA

In May 2020, I interviewed Dr Piyush Mehta, from the Dr YS Parmar University of Horticulture and Forestry. Located in the foothills of the Himalayas, in India's Himachal Pradesh state, it is Asia's second largest Government Agriculture University and is known for its research, and expertise in the socio-economic development of India's farming community.

Dr Mehta has been working at the forefront of agribusiness academics for the last 18 years and has published two books on agribusiness management, along with 35 research papers published nationally and internationally. He has led various research projects for the central government, and worked to enable organic farming among young agri-entrepreneurs in India.

1. **Do you think CSR has been successful across all sectors in India, in particular the agricultural sector? What do you think the challenges have been?**

I strongly believe in the benefits of corporate-led CSR initiatives, especially in a developing country like India, where there are large sections of society who face lots of challenges, striving hard to make a basic living. While there are many types of public development schemes and programmes available as solutions, they're steeped in bureaucracy and political agendas. This is why CSR in India is emerging as hope for the vulnerable people in society, where the larger earners within the country can make a difference, whether it's through their philanthropic nature or because it's a legal duty that is enforced.

Yet, in reality, I believe CSR is being carried out by very few sections in India's corporate world, because there's no proper scrutiny commission or CSR audit mechanism. Instead, CSR among the business community has become a way to gain kickback, earning tax holidays and accessing government subsidies.

Regarding the agricultural sector, CSR is invisible here because there's an absence of a good corporate presence in this sector. This is due to the fact that most of the agriculture industrial players are either medium or small holdings who don't have a deep pocket.

Though there are activities run by corporate foundations, which have had a positive impact in rural communities, there are not many examples of pure, business-led CSR initiatives. The ones that do happen are purely PR campaigns in rural areas, conducted by a few seed or fertilizer companies, who run education projects to empower young men and women, or rural employment generation, or the distribution of educational books to children. But these kinds of projects are rare.

The challenges that hamper CSR activities in India are many: there's lack of mass public awareness; there's no accountability over the strict compliance with CSR norms between state and central governments; absence of planning; and the lack of transparency in terms of the funds provided for CSR purposes.

2. India is the first country in the world to implement a national CSR law. Do you think this law has made a positive impact for the country?

It's probably too early to assess the impact of the CSR law, but we can see how it is being implemented in five states here in India, who have been very successful in leading CSR programmes. These five regions are Karnataka, Tamil Nadu, Kerala, Andhra Pradesh and Sikkim. These states have come out with their respective state laws for implementing and taking CSR forward in their respective areas.

Over the last few years, with a few amendments to the law, CSR is now being merged into a chain of various development projects, which previously was only handled by the government. Now, not-for-profits and government bodies, along with a public-private partnerships, have started to join the dots together, where CSR projects have started to reap positive results. Many of these are being witnessed in different parts of south India.

3. **Do you think this law makes India a CSR global leader? Could the rest of the world be learning from India right now?**

I believe that CSR can only work in its true spirit, if it is adopted rather than being enforced. Therefore, the government's CSR law needs to create a rationalized approach, embedding it within corporate culture – with better fund management, combined with operational transparency and specific objectives – which can then spur a real willingness among businesses to come forward to authentically operate and implement their CSR values.

Considering all these factors, India can still lead the world to speed up its development models based on CSR activities.

4. **Development of agriculture remains critical for India's economic growth, poverty reduction and food security, as over 58% of rural households depend on agriculture as their principal means of livelihood. From your experience, how critical is India's agriculture to its CSR initiatives with business and the central government?**

CSR is important to India's agricultural sector, where it can provide significant support for its development, by evolving technical knowhow, improving crop knowledge, increasing agricultural mechanization and more.

Agriculture in India is vital because of the demographic structure, which holds the largest sources of both employment and national income. Therefore, if an approach was taken where government banking and financial support is combined with corporate CSR operations, it can bring multiple results to the farming community at large. Plus, the vibrant cottage industries of India – such as handlooms and handicrafts, along with other types of sellers from the agriculture sector, which are now slowly being lost – will also benefit hugely from this integrated CSR-led approach.

5. What role do you think Indian businesses should be playing in shaping the country's CSR habits for future generations of entrepreneurs?

Until now, CSR has been led mainly by the top management teams at the big Indian corporate players, which has been a 'top-down' approach. What it needs is an integrated approach, where CSR is implemented by the entire company, with vertical and lateral thinking. Indian businesses can both influence and inspire this change and thinking in their approach to CSR.

Plus, Indian business CSR initiatives also need to benefit their employees, extending these values and activities to include employee safety, making better products to a higher standard and keeping business processes and operations greener and ethical.

6. How do you think the COVID-19 pandemic has impacted India's farmers, who are central to the economy as well as the CSR ecosystem?

Sadly, this pandemic has catastrophically impacted economies all over the world. However, looking at India's economy, which is based on its agriculture, the situation here is somehow a little bit more manageable. This is because, over the years, the country has worked hard to reduce its dependency on food imports, and been working hard to become sustainable, especially as it has its own large consumer base. Therefore, I believe India will be able to recover from this pandemic a little quicker than other economies with regards to its farming.

Also, over the last six to seven years, India's farming community has benefitted from the positive CSR activities from corporate foundations. And now, in the context of the pandemic, I'm hopeful that the corporate sector will come forward to intensify their respective philanthropic activities in a more substantial manner, focusing on public health and safety at large.

IN CONVERSATION...
WITH RUSEN KUMAR

In May 2020, I spoke with Rusen Kumar, Founder and Director of India CSR Network, the largest news network focused on responsible and sustainable business in India. Rusen is a respected media mogul and well known in the areas of social entrepreneurship, social journalism and social-economic development. He has been at the forefront in driving change for not only the vulnerable people in society, but also getting corporations to act differently.

There was no one better for me to speak to about CSR in India, a country that is one of the most powerful emerging economies.

1. **What is the concept of India CSR Network and what inspired you to start it?**
India CSR Network is a knowledge-driven organization that's bringing together all stakeholders in India's CSR and sustainability field. Our platform offers an opportunity for sharing best practices, laws, rules, guidelines, plans, policies, strategies, action plans,

awards, achievements, learning and training opportunities, case studies, publications, etc. We are the first web-based media house in India that writes and publishes across a wide range of issues related to social performance of businesses.

It was the absence of an online CSR and sustainability news platform that inspired me to start India CSR Network. I wanted to strengthen the CSR ecosystem in India and chronicle the change occurring within India's corporate world and their CSR activities. I was also being inspired by the rise of change-makers and business leaders doing great things. I wanted to 'bottle' this inspiration and spirit and share it with others, and an online media platform was the best way to do this well.

2. **Since you began, what do you think have been the biggest changes in India regarding CSR?**
The biggest changes have been a real shift in thinking, a new dawning where, aside from the CSR law coming into effect, companies have been investing in their CSR activities and working sincerely on CSR projects as their main line of business. Also, the compliance rate of companies has increased after the stringent reporting and the penal provisions that were introduced via law. Corporate CSR here in India has been growing at an exponential rate and it's becoming embedded in business behaviour, heading towards gradual maturity in India.

3. **Do you think the fact that CSR is law has had a positive impact?**
The law has made a significant positive impact. The successive governments have brought about incremental

change and made specific recommendations to change the guidelines by making CSR implementation, documentation and compliance more and more stringent and results-driven. In my view, this gradual change and growth will ensure that CSR is sustainable here in India.

I also think that this law can position India as a real global leader in this field.

4. Are Indian consumers becoming more conscious about their buying habits?

Yes! Indian consumers are becoming more and more conscious about their buying, lifestyle and eating habits. You also have to remember that India is a country of extremes – extreme wealth and extreme poverty – which means that it has two types of consumers. We're seeing that those in society who can uplift others are doing so, via their consumer behaviour, by making better sustainable choices.

We are increasingly witnessing a new pattern where consumers are empathetic towards responsible and sustainable brands.

5. What role do you think India CSR Network has in shaping India's corporate CSR habits?

I believe we have been playing an important role of promoting and celebrating good practices and inspirational stories by corporates.

India CSR Network is fostering connections and conversations between people working in this sector. It's by joining the dots that we can create positive change. We run workshops, conferences and awards, which helps encourage best practices and healthy competition, and furthers CSR excellence.

6. **How did the pandemic impact your platform at India CSR Network?**

The COVID-19 national lockdown impacted our platform in many ways. The positives are that the visits, views and the engagement on the website increased phenomenally. However, naturally, the corporates have been busy reorienting their overall strategy to survive and navigate themselves to re-emerge from this global pandemic.

We know that the pandemic has impacted the cash flow cycle, which has impacted the financial health of corporates and this has, in turn, affected our financials to some extent.

7. **What has your business strategy been during the pandemic?**

The pandemic came with opportunities as well. We here at India CSR Network believe there is now a greater emphasis on companies having CSR and sustainability at the core of their business strategy, rather than only charities investing in these values, and we've dedicated our editorial staff to this issue.

Lockdown gave us time to be retrospective and strategize. And, we're adding more features to our services, such as an online bookstore on responsible and sustainable business, an e-zine and a research unit.

Chapter 4

THE RELATIONSHIPS BETWEEN CSR & PR

THE BASICS OF PUBLIC RELATIONS

Now that we have an understanding of CSR, it's important to understand public relations (PR) – its elements, the benefits it can deliver and the role it plays with CSR.

Everyone seems to know the term PR, but not everyone understands what it means. Though many organizations recognize that it's a great way to build their marketing approach and their online reputation, very few know what PR involves.

PR is a component that can raise your company's authority, build relationships with key people and manage your reputation. It also helps to increase sales and attract customers. The aim of PR is to inform the public, including your potential customers, business partners, influencers, regulators and investors.

The essence of good PR is the ability to convey a compelling message that consumers, governments, media and the public can understand and follow. During the times of COVID-19, we can see the importance of correct messaging. PR needs creative ideas and thoughts, which are then communicated via traditional media and social media, including magazines, newspapers, television, radio and digital channels like Instagram, Twitter and YouTube. It's also about sending the right messages to the right places and people, to build your brand's reputation. It is a tool for all business types and sectors, whose main purpose is to raise the profile of an organization or promote a campaign/initiative.

Increasingly, digital communication is driving PR, where three important trends are affecting its future: social listening, digital storytelling and real-time marketing. In essence, this means there's never been a better time to be in business, an entrepreneur, an author, a start-up, a charity or any other kind of small- to medium-sized organization.

PR is a function that can change the future of your business. When used appropriately, it can 'make a company,' giving it the power to overcome almost any obstacle. PR is vital for any brand, and for many reasons.

BUSINESS BENEFITS OF PR

There are five essential benefits of PR. When done right, it can:

1. **Help Manage Reputation.** Any sort of business can face challenges, such as dissatisfied customers lashing out on social media. This is where PR can come in and help repair the damage. It can regain control of the narrative and change the way people think about your brand and business.

2. **Promote Brand Values.** In any industry, trust plays a key role in determining whether a business will be successful or not. PR work can increase credibility by improving an organization's reputation through various strategies and tactics, employing editorial coverage, press statements and social media programming. PR can send positive messages to your customers/audience.

3. **Strengthen Relationships.** Great PR means creating relationships with different types of media and influencers, and this ultimately helps grow your business.

4. **Enhance Your Online Presence.** In this world where everyone and everything is digitally connected, PR helps companies make the most of their online presence.

PR is generally focused on public opinion. In instances of an existing, fast-growing market, PR is becoming an important part of marketing communications. It influences the performance of marketing as a whole.

5. **Drive Leads, Sales And Profits.** Part of PR is marketing. When you enhance your reputation through a range of effective PR activities, you'll be able to reach new potential customers and clients, who will find more ways to connect with your business through your stories, press releases and online activities. PR will help you craft the right messages to resonate with your target audience, and then place your story with the right media. And now, with online media, this means people can click and buy.

PR AND CSR

The biggest reason some CSR initiatives fall short is that they don't feel sincere or genuine to employees and customers. This happens when the pursuit of marketing objectives is the main driver of CSR programmes. When businesses spend all their time focusing on how their CSR strategy will make their brand look great, they miss out on making moves that will actually impact the community and live up to the things their marketing campaigns are saying.

To avoid this, it's essential to know your brand and be able to tell your brand story in an easily understood way, using the mechanics of PR. Your story will need to have integrity and honesty, and when CSR is driving your story – because it is at the heart of your company – it makes the storytelling and messaging automatically authentic! This is the notion of CSR driving your PR campaign and strategy, not PR driving your CSR campaign.

CSR is not PR!

A CSR strategy that is part of your business strategy can do much more good for your company than great publicity. Therefore, before you get started on your PR plan and campaign, it's important to know who you are as a brand. This is where CSR is key.

Yet, many companies are confused about their own brand identity and values. If you don't know your brand, how can you expect others to know what you do and what you stand for? Many companies recognize the link between successful businesses and strong branding. They know that branding is not just a logo, or how their business is perceived externally, but too few realize that successful brands have their brand CSR values positioned at the core of their business. Ideally, branding is entwined with your CSR values, defining your business for yourself, your team, and your customers and other external audiences. It is the business 'identity,' embodying the essence of what it is, not just what it looks and sounds like.

Customers of all sorts of businesses are so savvy today that they can see through most attempts by companies to gloss, spin or charm their way to sales. When customers connect – because they share the same values and beliefs as the brand – it leads to better marketplace differentiation and higher sales, and encourages loyalty and advocacy. It can even protect your price when competitors roll out promotional discounts to drive sales. Your brand can also give you the ideal platform from which to extend your offerings.

During the pandemic crisis, we saw how brands that have CSR at their heart were able to still have a role, and engage with not only their customers but a much larger audience. These brands were visible – in a positive way – during these tough times.

CORE BRAND VALUES

Core values are the beliefs that your organization/brand/ company stands for, and serve as the compass that guides your brand story, actions, behaviours and decision-making. There will be times in business when you have to make tough choices, and your brand values can help navigate those challenges. Defining your core brand values helps define your brand identity and guides all your company's decisions.

The benefits of core values ensure that everyone within the business is going in the same direction, and helps you:

1. Attract better customers and staff

2. Know how to pitch your business to the media

3. Assess what kind of collaborations and partnerships you're open to creating and who you want to work with

4. Decide if you are a service-led business, and crystallize how and what you are selling

I believe that a business should not have more than five brand values, as five are easy to remember. Make them values that you believe in as a business person, and keep them simple. They'll need to be values that help define your goods and services, and always remember that people can see through anything that you're simply paying lip service to.

If you're able to get all the people in an organization rowing in the same direction, you could dominate any industry, in any market, against any competition, at any time.

The good news is that core values can help you achieve this! The bad news is that, in most organizations, if you ask four employees to articulate the company's core values, you get four different answers.

Some organizations have not defined their core values, while others set theirs years ago. But people and times have changed, so they do need updating. Start by brainstorming a list, and group similar ideas together, deleting those that are not essential.

Through discussion and reflection, you'll eventually get to a short, well-honed list. Make sure everyone in the business is genuinely happy with the core values. Once they are defined, announce them internally and use them; they're meaningless if they aren't used by everyone in the organization.

Here are a few tried and true thoughts on how to successfully create strong branding for your business:

- **Start by defining your brand.** Review the product or service your business offers. Pinpoint the space in the market it occupies and research the emotive drivers, rational needs and concerns of your customers. Your brand character should promote your business, connect with your customer base and differentiate you in the market.

- **Build your brand.** We're all made up of belief systems, values and purposes that define who we are and whom we connect with. These traits determine how we behave, communicate and act in different situations. When building a brand, it's vital to have this insight and understanding.

- **Ask what drives your business.** What does it believe in; what is its purpose? These are your CSR values, and they help establish your emotive brand positioning and inform the identity and character for brand communications.

- **Build long-term relationships with your customers.** Don't dress up your offering and raise expectations that result in broken promises. Instead, create trust with honest branding. Be clear about who your company is and true to the values that drive it every day.

- **Speak to your customers with a consistent voice.** This will help reinforce the business' character and clarify its offering, so customers know exactly what to expect from the product or service.

- **Don't mimic the look of big brands.** Carve out your own distinctive identity. There is now a big consumer trend towards independent businesses, and we've seen chains try to mimic 'independents' in order to capture some of the market. Truly independent operators can leverage their status to attract customers who are looking for something more original and authentic, which actually aligns with how they feel about themselves.

- **Be innovative, bold and daring – stand for something you believe in.** Big brands are bogged down by layers of bureaucracy, preventing them from being flexible and reacting effectively to the ever-changing needs of their customers. Those layers of decision-makers can make it hard for them to be daring with their branding.

- **Always consider your branding when communicating with customers.** Respect your customers' intelligence and allow them to find out more about your brand for themselves. This is the way to foster both engagement and ambassadors who enjoy telling other people what they've discovered.

BRAND STORYTELLING IN BUSINESS

Stories have been part of our lives since the beginning of time. Stories connect us and are the best way to teach, persuade and even understand ourselves. When they are emotional, we're more likely to remember and react to them. A compelling story, well told, grabs hearts and minds. In recent years, businesses have come to recognize the importance of storytelling. The advent of technology has advanced the power of the story, as technology is about sharing information, and sharing stories is a key component for personal branding and business success.

Storytelling is a business tool that can be used in different areas, from leadership, branding, PR campaigns and messaging to fundraising. We know that everyone loves a good story, and this can help you engage with people and get them to listen to you. In PR, your story will help you in many different ways, from talking to the media and fleshing out the 'about us' page on your website to enriching your social media channels. And, crucially, stories are the best way to distinguish yourself from the other brands in your industry.

To accomplish this, brands need to identify the unique story they can tell. CSR provides a credible, convincing story for a PR campaign, where businesses can reap the real benefits of this and tap into the changing face of news.

The most successful CSR initiatives are authentic, engaging and further the brand's mission. We know that consumers are savvy and can smell if something is not true, and with social media and the internet, you simply can't get away with making things up.

In brand storytelling, there are three important elements of a good story:

1. Make sure it's your story

2. Be authentic and real

3. Be engaging

Major brands like Lego and Coca-Cola and have become industry icons because of their fondness for storytelling. If you rely only on your products and services, you'll become just another brand that isn't able to differentiate itself from the others. You have to stand out – for the right reasons – with the right story.

CRAFTING YOUR BRAND STORY

This is perhaps one of my favourite quotes about a good brand story, and one that I often cite. Mark Truby, Chief Communications Officer for Ford Motor Company, said: "A good story makes you feel something and is universal. They want to grasp your values and your commitment to excellence; be inspired and intrigued. Storytelling is the most powerful way to convey these ideas."[20]

Armed with your brand values, you can start to create your own brand story. This story is about your passion for why you decided to start your business. It's why you do what you do. It could be a childhood dream, or a hobby that became an ambition. Start out simply, use easy-to-understand language and include descriptive words. Write your past, present and future story, and incorporate your brand values. Your brand story is not about selling, but about engaging, and it needs to resonate with your customers.

KNOW YOUR AUDIENCE

To successfully tell your story, you need to know who your customers are – whom you're talking to. This will help you plan where you want to pursue media coverage; what magazines you want to be featured in and what radio shows will have the right listeners for you.

Understanding your customer also means knowing how to engage with them and what their interests will be, so you're able to create tailored products, services and promotions. These are all elements in the PR mix.

Getting to know your customers is simple: you just have to talk to them, and you can do this through some basic market research. There are tools to help, some of which are free.

For instance, if you have a business website, Google Analytics is a great tool. It's free and generates detailed statistics about activity on a site. Google explains that the system "helps you analyze visitor traffic and paint a complete picture of your audience and their needs, wherever they are along the path to purchase."

Or, you can conduct an online survey, where you create a questionnaire, send it to your social media followers or email subscribers, and then quantify the results. To get people to participate in the survey, incentivize them with a prize or reward.

And, start to get to know your customers personally. This is one for more established businesses in particular. Take some extra time to get to know them on a personal level, remembering that PR is about relationships. Ask what they're concerned about, what appeals to them and what excites them.

DON'T JUMP ON THE BAND WAGON

Companies have begun to realize that personalization can make a real difference when it comes to connecting with customers. They're recognizing how important it is to have a real understanding of whether a trend is right for their business or not. Is the trend aligned with your core values, and can you authentically say that it's part of your business mission? Get it right and you'll build a foundation of trust and respect that will allow for real conversations with your audience. Get it wrong and you'll be lumped together with the countless examples that backfired, as happens so readily in today's digitally connected world.

Many businesses have learned the hard way what it means to miss the mark. You can avoid the hard way by doing these four simple things:

1. **Don't Piggy-Back.** Many businesses are making decisions hastily, out of the fear that they'll miss associating their brands with the current zeitgeist. The result is usually rushed, 'me-too' behaviour that's laughably see-through and hypocritical.

2. **Stay True.** You don't need to be everything to everyone. Be genuine, be honest, be real. To be credible, and taken seriously, you need to live by your values. Ask yourself what you can really own and defend.

3. **Be Brave.** Don't just talk. Do! No one expects bold statements on big issues that come out of left field and don't seem relevant. It's important that you choose a theme that's important to you as a business, aligned with the role you wish to play and the voice you want to convey. Proactively managing to move from the realm of talking to real-world action is key.

4. **Learn From Your Consumer.** You can't just sell culture. You've got to earn your place in it, and your business needs to engage with it purposefully. Businesses need to have conversations with real people, with real stories to share. This will provide the inspiration and understanding your company needs to make better decisions, faster.

CHANGING FACE OF NEWS

Once you know who your audience is, there are many new ways to reach them. We've seen growing reader and business interest in environmental issues and CSR initiatives, on a global level. Publishers are tapping into this and strengthening their efforts to cover CSR stories and initiatives.

Good News & Bad: The Media, Corporate Social Responsibility and Sustainable Development, a report by the UN Environment Programme, the PR firm Ketchum and the think tank SustainAbility, said this:

"The media sector could become the dominant industry of the 21st century. No other industry will so powerfully influence how people and politicians think about CSR and sustainable development priorities."[21]

In just the past year, a number of media outlets have launched sub-brands, newsletters, dedicated print editions and events that focus on this type of news. In September 2019, *BBC Global News* announced a new sustainability-focused sub-brand, *Future Planet*,[22] while *The Economist* launched a dedicated print issue on the climate crisis and Bloomberg Media launched *Bloomberg Green*.[23]

For the first time in its 176-year history, *The Economist* dedicated an entire issue to climate change topics such as rising carbon dioxide levels. Every section of the 21 September 2019 edition included an article on climate change, in addition to the cover, lead article and the 'Briefing' column.[24] The Economist Group has also been conducting marketing and commercial activities that have ranged from delivering the magazine to UK subscribers in a starch-based, 100% compostable bioplast film to offering New Yorkers a free coffee in an edible cup in exchange for plastic trash.

"It feels good to be speaking authoritatively about such a crucial issue," said Oliver Morton, *The Economist's* Briefings editor, who oversaw the special issue's climate coverage. "And it has been a great opportunity to remind ourselves – and I hope our readers – of something we are really good at: taking lots of terrific individual stories and bringing them together into something which is even more than the sum of its parts."[25]

Nic Newman, editor of the *Reuters Digital News Report*, has said that providing more coverage of - "the environmental issues "makes sense in general, but also increasingly in a business-to-business context as environmental considerations become so important to business."[26]

Meanwhile, ensuring that it is 'walking the talk,' *The Guardian* announced that it would no longer accept advertising from fossil fuel extraction companies in any of its publications. The decision is a bold move, especially as advertising makes up 40% of Guardian Media Group's revenue, which funds the journalism produced by *The Guardian* and *The Observer* journalists around the world. *The Guardian* believes many brands will support the action, and may very well choose to work with it more as a result. The paper noted that the future of advertising lies in "building trust with consumers, and demonstrating a real commitment to values and purpose."[27]

GETTING YOUR PITCH READY

To start putting all of this into action, it's first important to identify the elements of the CSR and PR strategy. These are:

1. **Knowing The Vision.** As an organization, when you put a vision and a goal behind your business strategy that is robust with CSR values, employees are able to get behind it and customers understand 'the why' along with what you are doing.

2. **Getting Your Staff Involved.** If your company truly cares about making a difference in the community, environment or workplace, your CSR strategy will allow employees to get involved. For smaller businesses, allowing your team employees to have a voice and support causes they care about, and enabling

them to pursue those causes, will give them clarity and confidence that you're interested in making a difference... even when nobody's looking.

3. Defining The Goal. This is a sizing of the impact your company is working towards through its CSR initiatives. It's important to steer away from always thinking about what these programmes will do for the profitability of the company. Your initiatives are not about the wonderful things you're doing for the world, but the difference you're contributing to and the impact you're making.

PITCHING YOUR STORY TO THE MEDIA

Once the above elements have been identified, you're now ready to speak to the media. In PR terms, you begin by 'pitching' your story to selected journalists.

Whether you're contacting digital or traditional print, TV and radio outlets, there are certain things you need to do in preparation, to get it right and help ensure successful coverage. When pitching to a major media outlet, they expect at least a unique angle, if not exclusivity. Be smart. Manage your story and your relationships. Here's how:

1. **Research.** This is the first thing to do, and probably the most important point of all. Understand the topic you want to talk about and do your research on it. Google, Yahoo and other search engines are your digital best friends – your go-to resources for anything and everything that's being said about your issue.

This research will help you define your angle and topline talking points before you make contact with a reporter. At the end of the day, media relations involves 95% preparation and 5% execution.

2. Identify The Relevant Journalist. This is a key part of your research: if you want to interest a reporter, read through what he or she has written previously on the topic. Find the byline of a journalist who writes on what you're trying to promote and reach out to that person. Being able to reference the writer's previous work is a motivator to get them interested in your story.

3. Prepare Your Pitch. Be sure the story angle you're proposing is a fit with the news outlet you're targeting. Double-check that it falls into the realm of what the radio show, news site, magazine, newspaper or TV programme actually covers.

4. Be Newsworthy. If you want to grab the news desk's attention and interest, this is key. If the editors and news team can relate your idea to a current, trending storyline, they'll be motivated to run with it.

5. Package Your Pitch. Draft a page about your business or organization that includes brief background and important proof points, along with two or three different story ideas. Your pitch is essentially an at-a-glance information pack to inform the journalist. Also, be aware of who you need to contact, and that there is a difference when it comes to pitching traditional print vs. digital media. At some news outlets, there are completely different editorial teams working on digital content and print material. Elsewhere, there are editors who work on both formats. This is why it's important to know who you're pitching to and what they cover on a day-to-day basis.

6. Email First. An overwhelming number of media prefer to receive email pitches before entertaining a PR call or a visit. In fact, many will only accept pitches by email, because it's less intrusive than being bombarded with phone calls amidst tight deadlines and competitive pressure. Don't waste their time by starting with pleasantries. Instead, use conversational, personalized writing, but be direct. Use your first 2–3 sentences to explain what you're pitching and why –zero in on the key point or angle. Say it up-front so the recipient doesn't have to waste time reading through to the end of the note.

7. Use A Clear Subject Heading. The subject line is the most important element in the email. Make it short and snappy. Many subject lines are too vague, and give no idea of the content, and this is when many journalists will delete a pitch before reading any further. Don't use clichés in subject lines, headlines or lead paragraphs. Avoid hype and exaggeration. Check your signature and ensure that it clearly shows your name, organization and other relevant credentials or affiliations. This helps recipients locate your email if they want to get in contact with you and talk about your story at some later date.

8. **State What's New.** You can safely use 'new' in subject lines if you're pitching a 'new survey,' 'new treatment,' 'new technology,' 'new app,' etc. Other good angles are the timeliness of the item, a compelling human interest angle, how unusual it is, the impact, inherent conflict, a well-known person or expert who's involved, a solution to a problem, a 'smarter way' or something that saves people money.

9. **Create A Connection.** Show that you're genuinely interested and share at least one authentic reason for working together. Don't get pushy, and if the journalist isn't interested, be prepared to move on and try another news outlet.

10. **Work TV And Radio Newsrooms.** Coverage is heavily dictated by the nature of the medium. For instance, TV relies on visuals and radio requires a strong spokesperson. The individual to contact for broadcast news and current affairs shows is the producer of each respective programme or the news desk. If you're pitching to radio or TV shows, some will decide to drop the interview into a programme. Check to see if your interview will be live or pre-recorded.

11. **Timing Is Crucial.** Find out the working hours of reporters and their deadlines, so you can ensure that your pitch and what you have to offer caters to their needs. Magazines are different from other types of media because of their lead times, as they plan much further in advance. In pitching to traditional print magazines, think at least 6–8 weeks ahead.

***12.* Keep It Real.** 'Real people' stories and interviews make any coverage come alive. If you have human-interest stories involving people who are willing to be interviewed on your behalf, put them forward in your pitch. Give a bit of insight into the subject's background, involvement and experience.

***13.* Don't Try To Sell.** No matter what you're pitching, don't push a product, an event or a business without a good hook – a compelling, attention-grabbing angle. From a PR perspective, your business takes a back seat to the actual story; it's the story that will get you TV coverage.

GREAT STORIES WHERE CSR HAS UNDERPINNED PR

Too many businesses and organizations still view sustainability as 'nice to have,' rather than integral to the way they do business. This approach is inherently bound to fail, and companies need to adjust to a new reality. A growing number of firms have just done that, and have truly built their brands on their CSR values. Their communications and PR strategies have been able to speak for themselves – the messaging is consistent, effortless and risk to the value of the brand is low. The following are a few examples.

TOMS Shoes is a brand founded on the idea that for every pair of shoes sold, the company will donate a pair to a child in need. Over time, the brand's mission has expanded to include providing more healthcare, education and economic opportunities to children around the world.

Since it was founded in 2006 in Texas, TOMS has donated more than 60 million pairs of shoes to needy children, restored sight to 400,000 people, provided over 335,000 weeks of safe water to communities, and helped 25,000 mothers safely deliver their babies.

Many CSR initiatives 'think local,' but TOMS Shoes made it a point to think globally. They integrated giving into the very core of their business model, which has helped to inspire not only their employees but their customers as well.

Warby Parker, an American online and storefront retailer of prescription eyewear that started in 2010, is another great example of CSR driving PR. The brand donates a pair of eyeglasses for every purchase made, and trains entrepreneurs in developing nations to perform eye exams and distribute glasses. This reinforces the true character of the brand: a commitment to giving back to society.

The French men's clothing label forlife, launched by brothers Lucas and Séverin Bonnichon in 2018, draws inspiration from the Patagonia apparel brand for its 'save the planet' business concept. They employ a one-product-at-a-time production model and, unlike the 'fast fashion' producers, focus on designing clothing to last. This sustainable brand further reduces its carbon footprint by crowdsourcing each design to prevent overproduction.

Sézane, a French women's clothing company founded in 2013, combines a vintage-inspired aesthetic with a forward-thinking, environmentally conscious mindset and commitment to giving back to the world. On the 21st of every month, a new design is released and 100% of the profits are donated to Sézane's philanthropic programme, DEMAIN. The company's holistic approach shows the good that can transpire when a shirt becomes more than an article of clothing.

IN CONVERSATION...
WITH VALENTINA ZAREW

I really wanted to gather a variety of strong, global voices for these conversations, and was thrilled to speak with Valentina Zarew, a PR and CSR expert based in Australia. She has worked with both large and emerging brands, including Mattel, Campari, Glenfiddich, Unilever, Woolworths, RedBull, PepsiCo, Australian Ethical, Marine Stewardship Council, WWF, Fairtrade Australia and New Zealand, to name just a few.

After first meeting Valentina a few years ago in London, we connected via LinkedIn and have stayed in touch. In 2012, Valentina, co-founded an award-winning communications agency, The Bravery, working with leading organizations focused on positive social environmental change. Since then, she has worked with H&M as Sustainability Manager for Australia & New Zealand and taken on an ambassador role with Textile Exchange. I spoke to Valentina for the book in May 2020.

1. **What are some of the classic joint CSR-PR fails you've seen over the years? In your opinion, how could they have been avoided?**

It's an interesting landscape for businesses as consumer sentiment shifts rapidly towards placing value on both the environmental and social responsibility of organizations. The increased media attention on topics such as climate change and supply chain transparency means consumers are starting to question their own values, and demanding that organizations are able to come to the table with these values in place when making purchasing decisions. In everything from superannuation to fashion, we now have what has been coined the 'woke' consumer.

The implication of this is that all organizations – small, medium and large – must take a magnifying glass to how they're acting as corporate citizens. Defining a pragmatic and impactful CSR strategy should be top priority, which is then implemented. I put the emphasis on pragmatic, as it is all well and good to reach for the stars and promise innovation, but you have to ensure that you can deliver. The starting point of an impactful CSR strategy is to either analyze and improve the existing foundations of the business, if you are an established brand, or embed social or environmental responsibility into the DNA of a new organization.

CSR should be holistic within an organization, and the CEO is integral when it comes to shaping, executing and reporting on the strategy. Leadership roles within each facet of the business should have an understanding of the role their department plays when it comes to sustainability. This requires close collaboration and communication lines within the business, that run between the CSR experts and function managers. Companies should take it on themselves to provide clear and accurate annual CSR reporting, and take it a step further by enlisting an independent auditor to verify their claims.

We have seen some major CSR and PR mishaps that essentially demonstrate the lack of cohesion between core functions. Whether it be lack of transparency, reporting or making false or misleading claims, these cause major and sometimes irreparable damage to a brand, resulting in decreased consumer confidence and commitment from employees. And, in some cases, they lead to the removal of executives in leadership roles.

Whether shareholders are formally structured into an organization or not, we need to commit to the understanding that every customer is in some way a shareholder of your brand, and interests must be handled with integrity. With every purchase, or with every recommendation to a friend or family, they're buying into the fabric of your brand – casting a vote, you might say.

2. **What advice would you give both new and established businesses on implementing their CSR strategies, and how they marry it up with PR? How can they avoid disasters?**

First, I would say that the brand needs to be genuine and transparent. The CSR programme should have a clear internal and external communications process so there's an opportunity for every individual within the organization to engage with it, and consequently become formidable ambassadors.

Second, when sharing information about the status of the company, ensure it is accurate and reflects the organization's true position, including goals, milestones, results and even challenges. More transparent communications, even when reporting on any issues and admitting to missing targets, results in stronger brand integrity. CSR is a discipline of continuous improvement and, when communicated in this way, a brand is able to easily and seamlessly bring both its team and customers on the journey with them.

3. **What could PR professionals and media teams be doing better when it comes to CSR and their communications strategies?**
Internal engagement and education between the CSR and communications department is key, as well as transparent reporting.

4. **Can you give an example of when you've seen CSR and PR work well together?**
A company I'm working with in Australia, called Spell & The Gypsy Collective, is a great example of a company that has integrated its CSR values of sustainability – 'People & Planet' work – into its communications. While the brand started its sustainability journey after they launched, it is a passion of the founders, who've instilled the same passion within the team, and has become a major part of the culture. From interrogating the supply chain to integrating more preferred fibres into the range, there have been some clear and quick wins, because the team adopted the values driven by its leaders.

The work speaks for itself and has become a talking point for the brand, which has attracted its community of customers, who align with its brand values. Spell takes it upon itself to report on the progress of its sustainability programme yearly by releasing a detailed impact report that scrutinizes key achievements, along with the challenges and the areas that can be improved. This report is audited by a third party to authenticate it, which adds to the overall integrity. This gives both customers and the employees confidence in the work that's being orchestrated, and aids the communications team with information that can be used along the way.

The communications team is able to use the results of the sustainability programme throughout its strategy, which involves traditional and digital PR. Some examples include gifting key influencers with products that exemplify the environmental and social work and developing digital content that's used to demonstrate how to style the products, which is also an educational tool. The brand also harnesses its social media presence to create discussions, such as using Instagram Live to interview its sustainability manager and founders, who answer questions from the community.

5. **What do you think celebrities should be thinking about when they agree to collaborate with the CSR initiatives of brands?**

My advice is based on two things. First, ask yourselves whether your values align. No matter how much you're being paid, if the product that you endorse does not align with your 'personal brand,' it means there's room for scrutiny, and the lack of integrity will be felt by your audience. Second, focus on the fit. Is it an authentic fit? Does this brand inspire you? Would you use and recommend the products and services to friends or family? Could this be a long-term collaboration? If there is a genuine alignment, then ask the brand for proof of any outward-facing claims to ensure that the brand is indeed living up to its word.

6. **We have seen a few social media influencers pay lip service to CSR, using it purely as publicity. How can we hold them accountable? Or, should they be holding themselves accountable and be better role models?**

This is an interesting question, as it can be a complex one to understand for those who are not professionals within the space. As a sustainability strategist myself, I can sometimes feel overwhelmed when it comes to navigating the landscape, because there really is no 'prefect' when it comes to CSR, and there can be many ways of looking at things.

The fact that influencers are engaging with the conversation – something that you and I, and many sustainability professionals, have been pushing for, for decades – is a positive. It shows that the movement has infiltrated popular culture. It's 'cool to care,' so to speak. Some influencers genuinely want to do the right thing, but might not know the right questions to ask the brand. I believe there is a place for brands to ensure that they are doing the right thing when they're developing their digital media strategy. Most communications professionals will have an understanding of what true and genuine alignment looks like, and by using these skills, it could keep both the brand and the influencer out of hot water.

The influencer's community might also hold them directly accountable. People are becoming good at sniffing out something that doesn't feel authentic or right, and social media is used as the way to expose the brand and influencer, holding them both to account. So, again, it's in the best interest of the brand to identify their talent accordingly.

7. **What do you think has changed in the last six years with regard to how the media reports on sustainability and CSR?**

A lot! First of all, when I was first working as a sustainability communications professional, a decade ago, it was extremely difficult to get the attention of journalists. Now, the landscape has changed dramatically, and it seems that rather than turning down a sustainability story, journalists are becoming savvier to greenwash and becoming more investigative.

8. **During the COVID-19 pandemic, we saw established brands trying to make a difference. Will both the media and consumers continue to expect companies to be doing more for social good?**

Yes. Thankfully, the market provides an opportunity to make changes and implement projects where our governments have failed or not done so. COVID-19 has not only challenged a brand's resilience, in their financial bottom line, but has also challenged their social moral compass. The fashion industry is a great example of this, where the media and advocacy groups worldwide exposed a range of brands that cancelled orders from their global suppliers with no intention of honouring their payments when the virus struck. This had major ramifications for the workers within the factories, as many of the garments were pre-ordered on credit.

What this meant was that suppliers had paid for everything from the raw materials to their manufacturing staff to complete the orders that brands placed months in advance. This issue got a lot of attention by the customers of these brands.

The pandemic has affected everyone in some way, and I believe that all of us – from CEOs of major organizations to those engaging with their products or services – will have been humbled by the impact that their choices have had on the fabric of society.

IN CONVERSATION... WITH FRED HUGUEZ

At the end of April 2020 I spoke to Fred Huguez, a rising star in inner-city Los Angeles politics who also has a strong business background. Fred founded L.A. City Kids, a charity that helps young people escape gang life through involvement in baseball. His journey has been a tough one, rife with personal adversity. He has come out of street life, having grown up in one of the city's toughest areas, where early on he crossed paths with violent criminal gangs, like the notorious State Street Locos. He fought the pull of gang culture through his love of baseball, and ultimately won.

1. **What was the reason for you creating L.A. City Kids?**
I grew up in Boyle Heights, in inner-city L.A. – a tough neighbourhood – where I lost 27 friends to gang violence. There were over 20 gangs in the community here. As a young boy I played baseball with my friends, and some weeks I noticed that we had fewer players than other weeks. I subsequently found out those not at the game were in a gang. We were a small community of friends, who were very tight, but were slowly being drawn into gang life; I kept away by playing baseball.

CORPORATE SOCIAL RESPONSIBILITY IS NOT PUBLIC RELATIONS

As we grew up, we all did not have enough. People told us to dream. We heard that a lot: 'Dream that you make it; you can be anything.' But we didn't know how – there was no one to show us or guide us, and we didn't have enough mentors at the time. We were also in a time where we were segregated in the community, where we couldn't go from one block to another without being chased or shot at by rival gangs.

However, today, I think that kids are lucky, because of the internet. It enables them to see outside their communities and be inspired. We didn't have that; we were just stuck. Plus, a lot of us came from foster care, where we had uncles or brothers and sisters raising us. I, myself, was raised by my grandparents. My mother was a heroin addict and I ended up with my grandparents at three months old. They brought me up and introduced me to baseball, which kept me entertained. My dream was baseball – I was such a big fan of the L.A. Dodgers (major-league baseball team) – and I didn't have time to get into gangs. It was at that time when gangs were coming into our lives; gang culture was everywhere.

Baseball was my salvation, and I have now looked to the game to help kids into a programme that allows them to dream of playing professionally. I believe it's my job to look after the kids in my own neighbourhood, making sure that they don't face the same things we had to. And, importantly, they have someone to guide and help them out of all that.

So, I organized my group and contacted the Dodgers. I did some fundraising, which enabled me to take the kids from the inner city to Dodger Stadium summer camp. It was such a great experience for me as an adult, and I wish I'd had same opportunity, but I'm so happy to see these kids play with the Dodgers. They're excited to be playing with the professionals.

From the summer camp, we then did the Dodgers Training Academy. This whole experience of playing baseball has improved their grades, inspired them and given them self-belief. All these kids have a sense of pride, which they didn't have before. Hopefully, we can keep them out of gangs, and they'll be playing all the way to college.

2. **Have your years in business helped you overcome obstacles to running L.A. City Kids?**
I was in the retail business for over 25 years and I was very successful, but there came a time in my life when I faced hardship. My partner was hospitalized with a terminal prognosis. My family and I went through this difficult time for two years, and it took its toll. Thankfully, we were blessed and my wife pulled through. That made me reflect on how I was spending my time. Being in business, I was so busy and I didn't have enough time for my family. I decided to refocus my life, which gave way to L.A. City Kids.

My business background helped me set up the organization, where I was able to draw on my business skills and knowledge. It gave me a voice to network, and confidence. I was able to negotiate with the Dodgers training centre and able to talk to sponsors, and that gave me the vision of how I wanted to grow L.A. City Kids. If I didn't have my business background, I would not have got L.A. City Kids off the ground.

3. **Would you like to see more corporates in America become more CSR-focused? Are local authorities and the federal government doing enough to support businesses in achieving their CSR goals?**

I don't believe that corporates in the US do enough, and I understand that a lot of them don't have the time. Some do give, and have lots of desire to do something. However, it makes a big difference when, as a CEO, you're involved, investing your time in a project. There's nothing like being hands-on as a CEO, because when you pass the buck to someone else, you can't guarantee it gets done.

Also, there's so much more that can be achieved when you're the CEO – you see what can be done, how the gaps can be supported and how to improve things. When you are in business, you have a better understanding of how to make things successful.

In an organization, it all starts with grants, and if you don't have the right expertise yourself – or be able to draw on that kind of knowledge, or be able to find the right assets or the right writer to help you complete the forms – it's tough!

Also, the money is hard for organizations like mine to access. But again, I was lucky. I was able to find my way around the system. Yet, for others it's not easy. Not only is fundraising hard, but a lot of organizations don't have the knowledge or support. However, if the local authorities and the federal government gave them that support, it would make the whole process easier for organizations.

4. **Is having a sustainable planet part of your political manifesto? If so, what would you like to influence to make the change both locally and nationally?**

Yes, it is. Growing up in the inner city, my neighbourhood was surrounded by freeways. The back yards for some of us is the freeway, where we're subjected to lots of smog and pollution. In those days, as children, we didn't understand how bad this was for us. I've noticed there are a lot of cancer deaths in my neighbourhood, and this was compounded in 2010, when my son was diagnosed with cancer. The doctors had no idea how he developed leukaemia.

It started to make me wonder about the relationship between air quality, and the smog we're breathing in, and how it affects us over time. I really want to create more awareness about this, and I would like to commission a study to research the smog and if there's a link with cancer. We need more studies, and this part of my agenda.

When I was running for Los Angeles City Council recently, I observed many things, particularly all the difficulties that I was running up against politically. I knew that I wanted to do things differently and took myself off the election. What I decided to do was look at what were the actual issues affecting the community, and what people needed, looking at everything from parking to the environment.

I've been looking at the elderly in society, particularly when we've been dealing with COVID-19 and the responses – how we're taking action and how long it's taking us. There are a lot of good people out there, doing great things.

Overall, I really want to be there for the people and actually do what they are asking for, making sure the seniors are getting what they need, making a difference for our children and recognizing these kids.

I want to do what the community needs and not just make political gains. So, I'm taking it one step at a time, playing my part.

5. **Are the children you're working with today concerned about the planet? Or, is this not a focus for them right now because they have other challenges?** I think for a lot of the kids – while I'm sure that the planet is at the back of their mind – they're dealing with other things, where their realities are about dealing with what's going on in their lives right now. They have tough challenges, where many of them live in single-parent families, where these single parents, mainly mums, are raising three or four kids. However, you would not even know about the problems they're dealing with, because they're always smiling when they're playing baseball. You can't see their troubles.

I heard about this one particular family. This young boy, he's in L.A. City Kids, and his mum, a single mum with three children, lives in a garage. They needed somewhere to live and I was heartbroken, because I know what it's like to be hard up. This boy has such great talent; I didn't want him to fall behind because of the circumstances he's facing right now. I know that this has a lot to do with your success later in life.

6. **How important is 'doing business with a purpose' to you and future generations?**

If I can accomplish my goals, which is getting these kids to college and see past high school – giving them a fair shake along the way, so that they have a chance to be the best at baseball or whatever their dreams are – then just that alone is going to be powerful. I haven't experienced that yet, but I can imagine when that does happen it's going to be something special! Getting them to college, that's my purpose, because I did not get there.

It's so easy to get involved in a gang, especially if your friends are in one. You get easily influenced, and if you lose a friend in a gang because a rival took them out, then that pain and anger fuels you into revenge for your friend. You find yourself going down the wrong path. But, if you have a mentor to support you and keep you on track, it helps. You're there when they're grieving for their friend. You can tell them that by making it, they're doing this for their friend.

Businesses can also be great role models, where corporates can make a difference. That alone is important for a minority growing up.

Chapter 5

#PRFAIL: WHEN CSR GOES WRONG

History is full of dark stories of companies abusing their positions of power, but society has put increasing pressure on firms to be socially conscious. In the age of the internet, it's much harder to hide errors and controversy, and so many companies have built their mission around the idea of making the world better.

We've all heard of Nike's hurdles involving sweatshops and not paying their workers properly in the '90s. Or the Nestlé baby milk scandal, where the brand targeted the poor in discouraging breastfeeding and aggressively pushing its baby formula in less economically-developed countries. Nestlé made it seem that their infant formula was almost as good as a mother's milk, which is unethical for many reasons. The two brands have never been able to shake off these negative stories, which pop up from time to time despite the good things they may have done since then.

A recent example was Burger King's special offering for 'Veganuary,' the movement to promote a vegan lifestyle for the month of January. Burger King marked the occasion by launching a plant-based hamburger, but its soya-based burger was being cooked on the same grill as the meat burgers, and couldn't be eaten by vegans. The story was picked up by the press and railed against on social media. The fast-food chain responded by saying that the burger was "for flexitarians and designed for people who want to cut down on their meat consumption, not cut out meat completely." Using an awareness month as a hook to launch a product that isn't actually suitable for your audience is just spin.

Meanwhile, the online apparel retailer Boohoo generated negative PR in the summer of 2020 with allegations that factories in the UK that supply the brand were guilty of worker exploitation. They allegedly paid their staff below the minimum wage and failed to provide proper protection during the COVID-19 outbreak. Following these allegations, which led to major investors severing ties with the brand, Boohoo ordered a full independent review of its supply chain, promising to terminate relationships with any suppliers found to be non-compliant with the brand's code of conduct. While a positive move, the company suffered significant damage to its share price and brand reputation that could have been avoided.

Actions that embody cultural intelligence and awareness are necessary when tackling any campaign strategy. Brands need to voice an understanding of the damage they can cause – and commit to doing otherwise – rather than try to justify their actions.

In the global marketplace, and the culture at large, audience is power. Consequently, keeping companies accountable for the way they use that power is increasingly in the hands of consumers. And this, inevitably, helps sculpt the relationship between companies and customers.

Conversely, tone-deaf publicity that signals a lack of culturally awareness and empathy can have an enduring negative effect. These are a few examples of activities that signal a CSR fail:

1. **Greenwashing.** This has become a familiar term for companies pretending to be interested in CSR to improve their bottom line. We know that people like to support companies that are socially conscious, so when a corporation greenwashes they're setting themselves up for failure. Feigning interest in social responsibility can have short-term benefits, but if – or rather, when – you're discovered, it can have a lasting negative impact on your reputation. Volkswagen provides a textbook example. VW's green initiative helped it become the world's leading car manufacturer, as people were convinced that its environmental standards were unmatched. Except, we were to learn, they weren't. As was widely reported, Volkswagen's cars weren't green at all. Instead, they were emitting pollutants well above the statutory limits and lying about it.[28]

Solution: Authenticity. The path to avoiding greenwashing is easy: be authentic. Don't claim to care about something you don't actually care about. Companies have a history of manipulating the public by claiming that they're leaders on an issue that people care about. These companies frequently get caught in their lie, but not before vast numbers of people are duped.

Again, this goes back to your core values – what you really care about. If you can't be authentic about social initiatives, choose not to engage in them. Volkswagen is learning the price of duplicitous greenwashing the hard way, with a ruined reputation and losses in the millions of dollars.

2. **Using Company Initiatives To Hide Or Avoid Controversy.** Companies often try to avoid controversy by pointing to their corporate social programmes. The idea is that people won't look at the problems lurking under the surface if you enact initiatives that do lots of good. While this is similar to greenwashing, what's important is how a company addresses an underlying problem when it's been brought to light. In some cases, better initiatives and a change in thinking are created after the veil of deception is lifted.

Solution: Owning Up and Fixing Problems. The best thing a company can do is face the problem head-on, constructively addressing situations when they're revealed.

3. **Not Showing The Big Picture Behind Your Efforts.** Some companies struggle to show how their efforts are working together towards a bigger purpose. While this isn't immoral, it isn't embracing the power of CSR. When company initiatives are focused on a particular problem or issue, it's easier to get people to embrace the movement.

Solution: A Coherent Narrative. A clear and compelling storyline can help describe what you're building toward, and help people embrace your initiatives. Establish the big picture behind your efforts and people will be more likely to support your work. You may be able to turn your piece of CSR into a social movement and lead the discussion on issues that are important to you.

4. **Fading Efforts.** Many company initiatives are born out of a desire to do good. They are started with the best intentions, and enjoy the greatest amount of publicity and support when they begin. However, over time it can be harder to stay true to the efforts you've put in place, fatigue can set in, and all of a sudden your initiatives are adrift and you've lost focus.

Solution: Consistency and Commitment. The solution to fading responsibility efforts is so simple

– build them into your business strategy. That way, they become effortless to implement and easy to sustain. Consistency and a dedication to excellence requires setting the vision so that others can follow. Through it all, you can forge a solid reputation as a company that cares about its actions and the legacy it will leave behind.

EVERY CORPORATE CRISIS EVOKES A SENSE OF DÉJÀ VU

Unilever, the multinational consumer goods company, has had its share of environmental and sexual harassment controversies. Following a lawsuit over mercury exposure, Hindustan Unilever in 2019 settled with some 600 workers from a now-closed Indian thermometer plant. The issue got wide attention from an Indian rapper's song, 'Kodaikanal Won't,' that modified the Nicki Minaj tune 'Anaconda' with lyrics about the mercury contamination. A 2011 *Irish Times* story exposed sexual harassment claims from African Unilever workers who said they had to bribe supervisors to stop unwanted advances. Unilever has since been working to turn things around by supporting the UN's Sustainable Development Goals and collaborating with grass root, not-for-profit organizations where its operating to improve the livelihoods of local communities.

Cotton On, Target and Kmart are among the fashion brands in Australia whose supply chains' working conditions have come under fire. The charity Oxfam Australia has asserted that the country's $23 billion fashion industry is guilty of "a system of entrenched exploitation" that sees workers in its Southeast Asian supplier factories paid as little as 55 Australian cents per hour. Since the Oxfam report,[29] Cotton On, Kmart, Target and City Chic have implemented measures to achieve a living wage for the workers in their supply chains.

Then there was the dreadful clanger by UK high street brand Whistles, the fashion magazine *Elle* and the feminist advocacy group The Fawcett Society. The three were caught in a scandal after *The Mail on Sunday* newspaper ran a story revealing that their collaborative 'This Is What A Feminist Looks Like' t-shirts were made in a Mauritian sweatshop by women earning 62 pence an hour.

A press release from Whistles at the time described the company's "shock" at the allegations and stated their commitment to manufacturing under "safe, fair, humane working conditions." A lesson learned from this incident is that anyone looking to use fashion to raise funds should conduct their own research into ethical practices. As long as there are journalists, campaigners and trade unions covering the garment industry, bad practices will be exposed.

Uber the ride-sharing app, lost its license to operate in London due to a lack of corporate responsibility. An essay published by former Uber employee Susan Fowler detailed a prevailing culture of sexism and sexual harassment at the company. It also faced a number of lawsuits in 2017 and investigations into sexual harassment. Uber took action to turn things around, appointing a new CEO, Dara Khosrowshahi, in 2017, and vowing to rebuild the company's internal culture and fix its broken brand.

And then there was the debacle at Wells Fargo, the multinational financial services company. It was revealed in 2016 that Wells Fargo employees had created 2.1 million fake accounts, without customers' knowledge, in an effort to meet quotas handed down from the top. The problems didn't stop there: in 2017, the bank revealed that the fraud was more pervasive than initially thought. In fact, employees may have created as many as 3.5 million bogus accounts. If that wasn't enough, Wells Fargo was also found to have charged over half a million customers for car insurance they didn't ask for and didn't need. As many as 20,000 of them may have had their vehicles impounded for defaulting on the unnecessary insurance charges. Furthermore, in October 2017 news broke that the bank charged over 100,000 customers late fees on mortgage payments when the delays were in fact the institution's fault. To turn things around, in October 2019 the company brought in a new CEO, Charlie Scharf, to sweep away the dirt.

In 2014, the cigarette maker Marlborough faced intense criticism for its 'Don't be a Maybe' marketing campaign. Critics slammed Marlboro's parent company, Philip Morris, for "breaching its ethical code" by targeting teenagers with adverts. The campaign included youth-oriented adverts that were regarded as a way to target a younger customer base. The photos that featured attractive young people travelling, climbing fences, partying and falling in love. Instead of apologizing, a spokesperson for Marlboro denied that its ads were designed to target teens. This generated even greater criticism online, and outraged anti-tobacco campaigners.

While Marlboro is not going to change, the World Health Organization (WHO) is responding to systematic and sustained efforts to attract a new generation of tobacco users. The WHO's annual 'World No Tobacco Day' is focused on creating public awareness to empower young people to engage in the fight against Big Tobacco.

Dove, the personal care brand owned by Unilever, is known for promoting positive body image through its 'Real Beauty' campaign, which depicts women of all shapes and sizes in a positive light. However, sometimes a brand can get it wrong even after getting it so right. In May 2017, Dove released seven limited-edition body-wash bottles in abstract shapes designed to resemble a range of female body types. The campaign went down like a lead balloon because the packaging sent the wrong message. Instead of reinforcing strong body image, critics claimed that it increased self-consciousness. In marketing, brands need to adhere to a strong and consistent sense of message or risk losing the confidence of customers, both old and new. Sophie Galvani, Dove's Global Vice President, believes these issues are part of being in the diversity "game"[30] and that at times they will be making mistakes, but that won't deter them from continuing to try to make a difference. Since then, Dove's 'Self Esteem' project has gone beyond advertising and into entertainment. It has collaborated with the Cartoon Network on popular children's TV series *Steven Universe*, where its characters discuss issues such as body confidence and bullying. The brand's purpose is to help the next generation with body confidence and is working hard to educate girls and young people.

IN CONVERSATION...
WITH TONYA FITZPATRICK

I met Tonya Fitzpatrick a few years ago at a conference in New Delhi, and thought of her when planning who I wanted to interview for this book. We spoke at the end of April 2020 – as the global COVID-19 lockdown was rolling out – and I was able to get her perspective on CSR and travel.

Tonya is a former White House appointee to the post of Deputy Assistant Secretary for Civil Rights Policy at the US Department of Education. She was also a delegate to the UN Commission on the Status of Women, an Explorers Club member and co-founder of World Footprints, a socially-conscious travel media platform. She's received numerous journalism awards, including from the Society of American Travel Writers, the North American Travel Journalist Association and the Caribbean Tourism Organization, as well as an African Community Service Awards honour and a nomination for a UN World Tourism Organization award.

Through World Footprints, Tonya promotes the transformative power of travel, with prominent guest speakers like the late Dr. Maya Angelou and documentary filmmaker Ken Burns.

1. What inspired you to set up World Footprints as a sustainable travel organization? What are your CSR values as a company?

I am a lawyer, and when studying law I had this determination to fight against social injustice. Social injustice irks me, and it was this feeling that inspired World Footprints. Now, as a travel journalist, I get to share the transformative power of travel and how travel provides an antidote to divisiveness. I also expose the things that are wrong, including waste, mistreatment of people and irresponsible behaviour towards our planet's resources. When my husband Ian and I started this company, we had the vision to connect people from different communities and cultures — to share our common humanity, history and experiences through the things that bring us together, like food, art, music, etc.

Our philosophy at World Footprints is based on the South African principle of 'Ubuntu,' which means 'I am because we are.' That is our common humanity. Ubuntu is about giving back, and at World Footprints we practice this through our stories and the connections we make. The words 'World Foot-prints' implies the footprints you're leaving on the planet, and for us it's the positive footprints, which is our value system. I want to live a passion-driven life and I know World Footprints is more than a passion project – it's my core.

2. Is there a common theme with social responsibil-ity, across all the different countries and regions you've visited?

There is the common thread of humanity, and a certain understanding about our environment and social responsibility. Yet, even with our shared con-sciousness, one of the most disappointing things I've seen on our travels was when we were on the island of Dominica, where it's been said that if Christo-pher Columbus was to come back today, it would be the only place that he would recognize. Because it's unchanged – still very lush and pristine. While there, we hiked a heritage trail and along that trail I saw rubbish strewn, and that really disturbed me because as islands they have had little development till now! I say 'till now' because the Chinese have purchased parts of the island and have started to shave off the sides of the island for development. We're also seeing how China is disrupting the lives of indigenous people in the Ecuadorian Amazon by drilling for oil. The governments of Dominica and Ecuador are allowing this to happen and I'm not confident that there's been any consideration given to sustainability or social responsibility.

That aside, I have seen wonderful examples of social responsibility. In the Colombian Amazon, deep in the jungle, two hours away from the nearest town, the 'camp' we were set up in had recycling bins! It was a surprise to see because that's something we're accustomed to seeing in urban cities. This left me with the question of whether this was a common thread, or how we as humanity have encroached on the planet.

3. **How important do you think it is for a company to have diversity within their CSR values?**

It is imperative! We all share a common humanity and we're all stronger for our differences. So, having different perspectives and ideas within a company is important. I make sure that within World Footprints we're sharing stories from a diverse group of people – from different gender and ethnic lines – representing what our planet looks like, because the planet does not have one colour hue, one height or body type or hair colour.

Similarly, I think a company that wants to reach a global audience needs to have the same approach and represent the global audience that they're trying to reach. There have been a few luxury brands recently, such as Gucci and Prada, who have got things wrong, and if they had strong diversity representation within their leadership at that time, these things would not have been signed off.

It's now more important than ever to have diversity within corporate culture, especially as this virus has given rise to increased xenophobia. Diverse voices or the lack thereof reflect a company's values.

4. **Have you seen any kind of change – whether negative or positive – in people's attitudes towards sustainability when you travel?**
Hmm... that's a yes and no. Yes in terms of other travellers who travel frequently, particularly travel journalists. Most already have sustainability ingrained as a value. As travellers we can see the difference sustainability makes when we compare places like Venice and Bangladesh, considered by IQAir and the World Bank to be the most polluted places in the world, to a very clean country like Iceland.

While the US is a country of excess, where food and energy waste is common, it's growing in sustainable consciousness. I've seen restaurants and companies voluntarily, or through a government order, do away with plastic products. For years, some hotel properties have been implementing sustainable practices, like giving guests the option to have their towels washed every-other day, and may have a recycling bin in the room. Yet, then they've not installed energy-efficient lighting or their restaurants may serve an endangered species. These approaches are not holistic, and for sustainable practices to be effective companies need to be all in.

Now, because of the pandemic, I believe attitudes have changed and are still changing. When we were in lockdown, here in urban America, where I live – which is a busy, built up area – I could hear birds chirping, which was beautiful. Before, they had been drowned out by sirens and cars.

I hope there's now more of a sustainable appreciation for our greener planet, where there's more of a consciousness about the need for responsible stewardship of our world. I think the way we've treated our planet and ourselves exacerbated the impact of the pandemic.

5. Have COVID-19 and the growing force of the climate-change agenda had an impact on World Footprints, not just in financial terms but with your mission to continue to foster a 'cross-culturalist' mindset?

I believe what everyone was doing during the height of the pandemic – restricting their travel but still having the need to create a connection – will continue. Travel has changed, and it will be different for a long time. We've seen people staying closer to home, or seeking out secondary and tertiary cities that aren't crowded. The bigger city breaks won't be that big a pull, and safety will be foremost in people's mind when travelling. People will be making their next trip count for something and won't unnecessarily take it for granted.

World Footprints did feel the pinch from reduced advertising and sponsorship dollars, but our mission to promote a healthier planet and connect cultures remains, and is a voice that people seek out. We've pivoted a little during the COVID-19 pandemic and started a video series called 'Connecting Across Social Distances,' which shared stories from around the world, putting faces to the pandemic that we were all experiencing. This video series supported our common humanity, and on the website we also posted articles about what travel might look like in a post-pandemic world. For instance, we interviewed someone from Thailand about the plight of elephants during the COVID-19 lockdown, as these elephants faced starvation because there were no tourism dollars to support their sanctuary. We also interviewed cities about how marginalized populations were being cared for during this time. No one was really talking about the homeless or the impact on the animal kingdom, so we did, because it touches on social justice and we want international perspectives and experiences.

At World Footprints, when we talk about sustainability of the planet, it also means for us to support the sustainability of humanity. We've seen during the pandemic, and disasters before this, that we cannot survive without each other. We remind people that we share more similarities than we do differences. We will continue interviewing champions of conservation.

We're still emerging from this global pandemic, and we hope that we can preserve the environmental benefits this mandatory pause did create, and remember how we were bonded by our common experience and how our humanity shined during that time. After all, we are one family and this is the only home we have.

IN CONVERSATION WITH...
FLORENCE KENNEDY

I stumbled across Petalon, a London-based online florist, who had me at bees! Founded by Florence Kennedy, Petalon gives 5% of its profits from bicycle deliveries to bee conservation and plants a tree for every 100 bouquets sent by carbon-neutral courier. All of the company's packaging is either recyclable or biodegradable. I managed to grab some of Florence's time and spoke to her in April 2020.

1. **What inspired you to set up a sustainable business, with CSR at the heart of everything you do at Petalon?**
We started on a complete shoestring. I used to work in sales for a consultancy that focused on trends forecasting, where I always came across these fantastic business models. I always thought if I had my own business, I would love it to have that kind of ethos, those types of core values, and still operate well and be a successful business.

We started small-scale and I didn't necessarily plan to be a green company, especially when dealing with the cut-flowers industry, because the industry itself is just not. The cut-flower trade is where the flowers have flown many miles and have had pesticides on them. I don't ever try to cover that up, and what we do is try and give something back to the environment, which is why we do the bee charity donations. Also, there are suppliers in our trade doing positive things, like the greenhouses in Holland that are so efficient that they give off more energy than they use.

We set out to do our best, and do what we can, well. Also, a lot of what we did, and still do, is because it works for us as a London-based business, and it would not have necessarily worked for us in another city, country or region. It all started with how we can do our bit, and these aspects made sense for us.

It's about looking at the good stuff and being responsible. This remains at the business's core and is also the kind of lifestyle that we want to achieve too. The business is an extension of our lifestyle. We evolved as a business, which has been driven by our personal passions and commitments to the planet. We wanted to be open and honest with our brand values – what we're trying to achieve.

2. Has being a CSR-led business made it easier to tell your brand story to the media and customers?

Yes, and it's something that we're constantly trying to improve and enhance. It's also about getting on with your game and not necessarily seeking out PR, but working towards being the best you can be. Our story is at the forefront of everything we do, letting people know what we do clearly.

We are all for being open and honest, and I'm all for listening to our customers, who give us suggestions. We have such a great community of customers, who add value to what we do and help us find solutions to some of our business needs. We are very transparent with our clients and they respond to us.

We really know our customer and community, which is a very female community, which itself is very interesting. Particularly with our recent crowd-funding campaign, where over three-quarters of our investors have been women. Our return rate is fantastic and we're very lucky with our customers.

3. **What have been the business challenges of starting a conscious-led business? And, how should government and local authorities be supporting businesses like yours?**

It is hard, as I don't particularly feel that we have had that much support. But then, we didn't let that deter us, and we kept our heads down to keep going. The best thing that I did was join an initiative at the British Library, where they have an 'innovation for growth' scheme. It's free, with certain criteria for joining. We joined and got time with different experts, from branding to IP lawyers, which was really useful, and you're also able to meet other types of London businesses. Otherwise, there seems to be no business support that is CSR-led or focused.

There have been challenges, like you would find in all businesses starting up, but we are very proud, as it has given us an income over the last six years.

During the pandemic, it had been an uncertain time, where we had our local and overseas staff return home, leaving us with less staff but triple the orders! My husband and I were able to keep things going, which was great, as we looked at the way we had been doing things. As a result, we improved our processes and managed to run the business efficiently, at a much higher volume than we were used to. It has been daunting, but we'll emerge from this a stronger business.

4. **Do you think consumers are looking for more businesses with an ethos like Petalon's?**

I think it's easy to get trapped in your own bubble on social media, with people who have the same outlook as you. Saying that, customers find us and buy from us, because they do like the concept and what we are doing. We always receive a lot of wonderful feedback from our customers; it's not that we even chase it or ask for it. People just take the time to give us feedback about how our bouquet of flowers has made a difference to someone.

We're very transparent and I think that's what customers like. They know what they're getting.

5. **Do you see us as a society that will appreciate nature more, after the COVID-19 pandemic, and do you think this will have a positive impact for your business?**

I think it depends on where you are based and your economic circumstances. We saw during the UK lockdown that those people living in high-rise flats craved being able to walk in a park and have some greenery, while those with big gardens were appreciating their own gardens more, because they were spending more time there. It's been different for everyone and has affected our lives in different ways. Did you try to buy flower or vegetable seeds when the lockdown started? Those sites had a shopping timer on them because they were so busy! People wanted to grow things. Whether it was growing vegetables or their own flowers, people were planting, and that's been a good thing.

During the lockdown, I listened to podcasts that discussed the 'power of flowers,' where there is evidence of how flowers can lift your mood and can provide happiness. So, now, whenever I'm packaging our bouquets, it's nice to stop and appreciate that we're making a difference.

COVID-19 has given us a shared sense of responsibility. It's like we were all grounded because we had been misbehaving and not respecting the planet. During those times there was a sense of community and togetherness, where lots of initiatives of giving back were happening, more than before. That, to me, has been a positive.

6. **Who are your business leader role models, who are supporting the environment?**
I like brands with a clear founder, who are doing new things, and there are a couple of companies who are doing things differently. I just love it when they're open about their failures. It's so refreshing. It takes down that façade that things are easy, and instead says that things can be gritty. Especially when, as a business, you're trying to give back to the environment. You may not be making any profit. So, you have to rethink things.

Finisterre is one of my favourite brands. They started off humbly and are surfers themselves. In the beginning they were trying to create a warmer wetsuit for when they got out on the cold sea, which evolved to how to use better materials without micro-plastics. Being surfers, they are connected to the sea and wanted their business to be better for the ocean. They are looking at the science of how to reuse plastic waste from the ocean to make fabrics. They're doing lots of exciting and innovative things.

They started off small and now have stores in quite a few major UK cities.

Another one is a small skincare brand called Haeckels, based in Margate, UK. Again, they're open about the things that work and have not worked. They are doing exciting things, such as their packaging, which is infused with seeds, from which plants can grow. Again, they're very different and innovative and think outside the box when it comes to being more sustainable.

Chapter 6

WHEN CSR WINS

When brands and business have not been led by their brand egos, but with their CSR hearts and commitment to the planet, that is when success happens. CSR lends itself to good news stories and is an abundant source of positive PR.

CSR is definitely based on a sustainability mindset. Yet, it is especially based on what companies can do to help reach a sustainable development path. However, there are other circumstances under which we can act in a sustainable way. These range from the way people use technology to the food they eat and the modes of transportation they use. The clothes people buy, how they organize their houses and their consumption habits are also related to sustainable and responsible behaviours.

A commitment to clear communications from a trusted spokesperson is a must. We can see many brands and organizations waking up to this, and wanting to do it well, and we can learn from them.

One of my favourite discoveries is the Kavli Trust, which grew out of Kavli Holding AS, a Norwegian cheese wholesaler founded in 1893 that's had international success for more than a century. Founder Olav Kavli's son, Knut Kavli, shared his father's social conscience, and established the Kavli Trust in 1963 to secure the long-term future of the company. The family's vision was well ahead of its time, ensuring that CSR values have been imprinted in the DNA of all its brands. The trust owns the dairy product company Q-meieriene and other socially responsible businesses in Norway, Sweden, Finland and Great Britain. For example, its Primula Cheese brand in the UK dedicates all its profits to supporting research, humanitarian and cultural projects to improve people's lives. This means that every time you buy Primula Cheese you're supporting worthy causes.

The Lego Group, the Danish toy brand, has been on the top-10 list of most reputable companies in the world for the third year in a row. It has a strong, steady presence as it builds a coherent storyline with its values of sustainability, education and societal contributions. Using innovation, Lego replaced its plastic materials with plant-based substitutes derived from sugarcane. Another particularly respected company is Rolex, which has been one of the top ten most reputable companies in the world for four consecutive years. The Swiss watchmaker has an impressive record of over 40 years of philanthropic work, investing in social enterprise projects. It sponsors projects that focus on innovation in distinct areas: Science and Technology, Arts and Culture, which makes sense for a company with a reputation as an innovator in watchmaking.

Welcome, Netflix! It's a company that has kept positive conversations focused on its business expansion and subscriber base growth, developing an image of innovation. Netflix's positioning on issues has set it apart as a positive disruptor in the mainstream media and film industries. By removing actor Kevin Spacey, who'd been accused of sexual impropriety, from House of Cards, one of its top shows, the company sent a clear message about its priorities. Consequently, Netflix seems to have gained a fairly strong reputation for ethics.

Another industry hitting the spot is the beauty sector, which has a plethora of products based on CSR values and sustainability. The changes there are being driven by consumers interested in reducing their carbon footprint and protecting the environment. Companies big and small in this field are stepping up their sustainability game, prioritizing the responsible sourcing of ingredients, implementing earth-friendly manufacturing processes and experimenting with inventive recycling programmes. Mega-brands are making major changes. L'Oréal has committed to being deforestation-free by the end of 2020 and Estée Lauder is working closely with the global non-profit Roundtable on Sustainable Palm Oil to ensure that their cultivation methods and sourcing have minimal negative environmental impact.

Music brands have also aligned themselves with sustainable values. The rock band Coldplay pledged to make any future tour 'actively beneficial' to the environment. Front man Chris Martin told *BBC News* in November 2019 that the band was waiting to tour in support of its new album, 'Everyday Life,' so it can ensure that the tour is carbon neutral.

"Our next tour will be the best possible version of a tour like that environmentally," said Martin. "We would be disappointed if it's not carbon neutral. We've done a lot of big tours at this point. How do we turn it around so it's not so much taking as giving?"[31]

Coldplay's just one of the musical acts to address sustainability. Singer Billie Eilish has announced plans to make her world tour "as green as possible" by banning plastic straws, encouraging fans to bring refillable water bottles and providing comprehensive recycling facilities. A feature called the 'Billie Eilish Eco-Village' was set to be at every venue on her 2020 tours, where fans could learn about their role in the climate crisis. Those who pledged to fight the climate emergency with the organization Global Citizen could earn free tickets to the sold-out shows. However, due to the pandemic, things have been put on hold.

The rock band The 1975 is working to make its tours carbon-efficient, and has pledged to plant a tree for every ticket sold for a planned UK arena tour in February. Plus, the group stopped producing new t-shirts, instead of screen-printing a new design over old merchandise stock.

NEW BREED OF CELEBRITIES

There has long been a relationship between celebrities and PR, especially in today's celebrity-led culture. Stars have the power to generate interest, excitement, and appeal to consumers. Many brands clamour for the clout of a well-known actor, actress, musician or model to be a part of their PR campaigns. Consumers take note of public figures and their activities, and remember celebrity endorsements, leading to brand awareness. This increases a brand's odds at the next purchase.

Yet, there's a growing trend of celebrities no longer just lending their names to causes, campaigns or charities. Instead, they're starting their own socially-responsible companies and initiatives to help tackle some of the biggest social and environmental problems.

Oscar-winning actor and film producer Leonardo DiCaprio, who's known for being passionate about the environment, founded Blackadore Caye, where he's building a ground-breaking, sustainable resort on a private island off the coast of Belize. The project focuses on restoring the island's natural resources instead of merely raising awareness around environmental issues and eco-living. It will feature homes and villas built with sustainable local materials, integrating renewable energy, electric vehicles and innovative water and waste treatment systems. In an interview with *The New York Times*, DiCaprio said about the eco-resort:

"The main focus is to do something that will change the world. I couldn't have gone to Belize and built on an island and done something like this if it weren't for the idea that it could be ground-breaking in the environmental movement."[32]

Grammy Award-winning musician, fashion designer and entrepreneur Pharrell Williams is the creative director and co-founder of Bionic Yarn, a company that creates high-performance yarn and fabric from recovered plastic. The company has teamed up with some of the biggest names in the apparel, including Adidas, Timberland, Topshop and GAP to create upcycled clothing collections. It also recently collaborated with jeans brand G-Star Raw and the non-profit Parley for the Oceans to transform plastic recovered from shorelines into an entire denim collection.

Matt Damon, the actor, film producer and screenwriter, is ranked among *Forbes* magazine's most bankable stars and is one of the highest-grossing actors of all time. Damon is one of the co-founders of water.org, a charity that provides safe water and sanitation for communities in need. It also has an initiative that provides small loans so more people can gain access to clean water. In addition, its New Ventures Fund provides money to innovative projects working to solve the world's growing water crisis.

Celebrities who are serious about making a difference can be powerful drivers of social change. They often work with like-minded organizations, but the emergence of celebrities who aren't simply the faces of, but the creators behind, social businesses is an interesting trend. These types of celebrity-led social enterprises are slowly becoming part of the CSR sector and are having success.

DURING THE COVID-19 TIMES

During the global crisis, many businesses reacted quickly, pivoting faster than national governments. Responses from some brands and companies were particularly bold, with notable examples of businesses tapping into their core values to make a real difference, and not just seeking publicity. Even though the private sector was very stretched during this time, the balance between businesses doing the right thing versus the wrong thing was important.

In a survey conducted by the PR and marketing consultancy Edleman in March 2020, they found that respondents in eight countries – Brazil, France, Italy, Japan, South Africa, South Korea, the UK and the US believed – 'my employer' is seen as better prepared to combat the virus than 'my country.' Some 62% of respondents said they trusted employers to respond effectively and responsibly to the virus.[32]

The World Economic Forum joined with the WHO and other partners, including Edelman and the Wellcome Trust, to create a COVID Action Platform. The online resource included a COVID-19 transformation map, which companies could embed on their websites to enable employees and other stakeholders, providing one-click access to the latest strategic trends, research, analysis and data.

The following are some of the businesses that have fought the good fight against COVID-19, working to 'do right' by their customers and employees. They've been socially useful and relevant in all that they do, and can proudly say that they were a force for good in this global war.

The independent UK brewer BrewDog made hand sanitizer at its distillery in Aberdeenshire, amid shortages driven by coronavirus fears. BrewDog's founder, James Watt, announced the retooling on social media: "We are determined to do everything we can to try and help as many people as possible stay safe," he said. The company said it was "working around the clock on producing the first batch," to be given to local charities and the community rather than sold.

In India, the food and restaurant app Zomato launched a public donation initiative to fund food 'ration kits' for some of the country's 450 million daily wage earners who lost their incomes. The scheme, which is being rolled out across 26 cities, raised ₹80 million ($1.07 million) in its first two days.

The pandemic also galvanized the tech sector, which tapped its core competencies to help in the response. Examples included The Bill and Melinda Gates Foundation, the Microsoft founder's philanthropy, which donated $50 million towards the development of a vaccine, and social media giant Twitter, which pledged to remove disinformation about COVID-19 from its platform.

The UK pharmaceutical giant GSK donated $10 million to the WHO to support its work to detect and manage the virus. It also made available compounds from its library to help a collaborative research project, led by the Bill and Melinda Gates Foundation, to accelerate therapeutic solutions to the virus. Unilever provided free soap, sanitizer, bleach and food valued at €100 million. Around half of this donation was distributed via the World Economic Forum COVID Action Platform. Unilever also provided $500 million in cash flow relief to hard-hit suppliers and small-scale retail customers in its value chain.

And, as BrewDog did, other companies repurposed their resources in response to the call for essential health products and equipment. UK engineering firm Dyson adapted its digital motor technology to design and produce a ventilator for use by the NHS. In the US, GM and Tesla both pledged to do something similar, while Ford worked with 3M and GE Healthcare to help produce respirators, face masks and other medical equipment.

On the celebrity front, Lady Gaga teamed with the WHO and Global Citizen to produce and appear in a televised concert to benefit the COVID-19 Solidarity Response Fund. The 'One World: Together At Home' event, in April 2020, included virtual performances and appearances by Mick Jagger, Elton John, Billie Eilish, Lizzo, Chris Martin, Paul McCartney, Stevie Wonder, John Legend, David Beckham, Idris Elba and others. The programme was hosted by talk show hosts Jimmy Fallon, Jimmy Kimmel and Stephen Colbert and carried by a host of international broadcasters.

The purpose of the virtual concert was not fundraising, but to tell the stories of and celebrate front-line emergency response communities, healthcare workers and their acts of kindness. Lady Gaga said she wanted the event to "celebrate and encourage the power of the human spirit." Separately, the Oscar-winning singer and actress helped raise $35 million from several global companies to benefit the response fund.

Corporations have the power and responsibility to lead the way and create large-scale consumer behaviour change, while dramatically improving manufacturing standards. The influence of brands and the messages they communicate to people, can drive them to participate in solving the challenges surrounding them. Meanwhile, on the production side, pressure from corporations has in many cases improved the way factories are built and operated, benefitting both employee welfare and environmental protection.

IN CONVERSATION... WITH PETER COBAIN

Just before the UK went into official lockdown in March 2020, I interviewed Peter Cobain, co-founder and CEO of Trio Sana. This medium-sized family business in the essential oil trade is a UK Soil Association certified organic grower of Roman chamomile, German chamomile and lavender on its stunning 40-acre Inglenook Farm near Liverpool.

Working with a resident biologist and business partner, the company distils natural ingredients into the highest quality essential oils for sale globally.

Everything at Inglenook is underpinned by sustainability and is CSR-led. The farm produces a range of handmade beauty and health products on-site from these naturally-sourced ingredients, which are available at the farm and through its online shop. The farmhouse café serves freshly-prepared food from locally sourced ingredients, while the retail shop sells local honey and local artisan products. If that wasn't enough, a number of local craft businesses operate at the farm, including a bakery, a vintage cycle sales and repair shop, a photographer, wood carvers and wedding planners.

1. What inspired you to establish a business with strong sustainable values and CSR initiatives?

Trio Sana began from our farm – Inglenook, in the northwest of the UK – where we grow and distil organic crops. This organic path was already part of where we were heading as a company in terms of CSR, and integral to our operations.

In 2018, during a month-long visit to one of the harvesting regions of frankincense, which was in Somalia, we had the opportunity to live and speak with the communities, who had so little, but were willing to give a lot. It was clear to us that the current practices within the supply chain needed a new approach – to think and act differently. We were clear that we wanted to supply frankincense and myrrh oils, and resins that were organic-certified through ECOCERT (a certification group) and include Fair For Life (fair trade) accreditation. We wanted to be sustainable, ethical and operate a company for organic essential oils, with CSR values at the heart of our business model.

2. Does Trio Sana do business differently from other companies similar to yours because of your CSR values?

At Trio Sana we do business differently by ensuring that it is directly involved in the supply chain from beginning to end: from harvesting, documenting the harvest and working with the individual communities, to training the harvesters, sorters and packers in the requirements of organics. We want to be transparent, which is also demanded by the FFL accreditation.

Crucially, for us, the important factor is for the wider international buying community to purchase the oils from us, so we can invest funding from our profits back into community projects where these raw materials come from and ensure that a fair price is paid for the raw materials. It provides a stability in the purchase of the raw materials and the sustainability of the frankincense and myrrh trees. An added benefit is that it assists in the education of these harvesting communities.

3. What have been the business benefits for Trio Sana from being CSR-led?

The business benefits have not been that straightforward, as this is new thinking and a new approach to the industry. Currently, the international supply chain requires quality oils at the cheapest price, to ensure that there's maximum benefit for the business-to-consumer entities.

What we need is a stronger awareness campaign for consumers, to help them understand that when buying an organic and sustainable-based oil, they are also receiving a high-quality product at a fair price that is being passed directly to the communities growing and harvesting these oils, which can improve the lives of these farmers.

While the organic and sustainable story is important, we still have a long way to go before we can make a real difference. But things are happening, and there are now more conversations and questions being asked about our oils, how we ensure the quality and the supply chain process. This is a big improvement, as not so long ago, buyers were not really interested and only wanted to know the cost.

4. **What have been the challenges to a business like yours, that's CSR-led?**
The challenges have been through the entire supply chain, in getting the communities to understand the requirements of the processes. Bringing an organic and fair trade-certified product to market is a new concept, and it will take time to break into the buyers' market. It has taken us two long years and we've only now received our first main order, which is from the USA.

While buying companies like the 'story' that goes with the oil, it's evident that their end clients have no requirement for these certificates and accreditations. Understandably, the farming communities want regular orders for their resins and are frustrated at the slow progress. We both feel and understand their frustrations and know that it all comes down to perseverance.

Our biggest challenge has been to keep the company viable, during times of slow sales of the oils. There have been tough times, but we know and believe that we're doing the right thing and it will work for us in the end.

5. Supply chains are important for all businesses. How do you regulate the supply chain for the oils you source for Trio Sana?

We have a rigorous supply chain process for our own frankincense and myrrh oils, including checking the resins ourselves prior to purchase and witnessing the resins being packed and labelled. We photograph the whole process and then re-verify the packages when the containers arrive at our distillery. We also take resin samples and distil them for analysis, so we understand the oil profile prior to distilling the resin.

The whole process, from harvesting through to export/import, is conducted under the ECOCERT processes, and in the UK through our own quality management system and the Food Federation certification. We only work with one broker, who we trust and have a long working relationship with. The broker fully understands the importance of being organic and ethical.

6. What are your concerns for the planet as a business leader, and what would you like to see more businesses commit to do?

We all live on this unique planet, where we all have a responsibility to it and our future generations. It's important that we all work together to ensure that the ecosystems remain in balance. Raw materials must be produced in an ethical and sustainable way that supports the communities, including the balance of the regional ecosystems. By working together at a macro level, this will support the larger systems that affect our planet.

A focus on sustainability is a must for all, whether growers, producers, retail or end users. There are many natural products in the market that emanate from finite resources. These must be very carefully managed by the whole supply chain, and excess profit cannot outweigh the risk of losing a natural resource forever.

7. Do you think the way global leaders responded to the coronavirus outbreak has parallels with efforts to limit global warming, and that they should be listening to science on that as well?

At the time, there was a different response to between COVID-19 pandemic and global warming, because the virus was 'here and now.' Therefore, what is real and affecting me today and tomorrow means that I must take action to survive personally, and to ensure my business survives.

Global warming is happening, and we need to take action to reverse or help slow its effects on humankind. Business leaders need to balance the demands for profits by shareholders and to recognize the need for change, which is also being driven by the public.

The biggest issue is at the international governmental levels and cooperation. Where governments on the whole want to be seen as the leaders saving the planet, in reality, they will have succumbed to the large corporations, who need to feed the shareholders.

COVID-19 has, however, made some governments, corporations, small- and-medium sized businesses and people re-evaluate how they are operating and living. This, we hope, will have a positive effect, towards more organic and sustainable products – and the rise of more CSR-led companies – but only time will tell if this happens.

IN CONVERSATION... WITH VINCE SCUDDER

In June 2020, I spoke with entrepreneur, philanthropist and business owner Vince Scudder, who I met years ago at a business conference in L.A. We gravitated towards each other, with our British sense of humour and our own core values. Vince is one of those business leaders who probably has a drawer full of those 'seen that, done that' t-shirts! He has a great business mind, and a knack for making money – which is what many of us want – but also a focus on how to do that ethically and with real core values. He's currently Group Director at MG Cannon Ltd, a UK car repair business with ten locations.

1. **Did the COVID-19 pandemic highlight the importance of being true to your core values when you were collaborating with other businesses?**

Yes, it did. And it was not easy making long-term decisions. We had to create a process of getting staff back to work, when at the time we didn't know who would still be there to deal with or what the economic landscape would look like.

However, saying that, in 2019 we had started to review our core values as a company, as we felt that they needed re-evaluating, and wanted to align our core company values with our personal values. It's important for directors within a company to be aligned with their own values. They need to be the same values; they just need to complement each other.

My own core values are around trust and respect. I've always felt, even before core values became fashionable, that they are important, and my one reason for being in business is to create wealth. This then flows down to those people in and around the business – the people I employ, my family, and so on. It's not just about trying to become a multi-millionaire. The more I can create wealth, the more I help others, and this is how this money is distributed to help those around me.

I believe you can create wealth with integrity, ethically and in a sustainable way, without compromising others. You can make a profit with values. Past experiences have shown me that you can do the right thing, treating people properly, and have good relationships with your work and supply chains.

Can you do it ethically? Yes, you can. Do you have to make compromises? Sometimes, yes you do. These are the decisions you'll need to make as an entrepreneur, as a business owner or leader. It's about balance and compromises. It would be difficult to say that I am saving the planet, as one of our businesses is repairing motor vehicles. Yes, there are electric vehicles out there, but I don't think they have the best carbon footprint, that people think they have. I'm also dealing with diesel and petrol cars, and I am promoting keeping them on the road. While that is not climate-change or socially responsible – some people would have a view on this – it is very much about doing business better and considering the ways to do that.

Once we all fully emerge from this pandemic, I believe we won't go back exactly to where we were, but we won't be that much further ahead regarding how businesses act regarding CSR values.

2. Will you be strategically realigning your business model to partner with other businesses that act and behave with core values?

We have already been having conversations with our supply chain, both on the sales and purchasing sides, and we're beginning to realize who has CSR values and who doesn't. You gravitate to and want to do business with those who share the same values and understand that we are all in this together. During the pandemic some of our business partners were fabulous, while some were not so helpful... and, well, you vote with your feet, don't you? At the start of the lockdown in the UK, I believe the government was brilliant during this time for businesses here.

For instance, we have three types of clients: the company that leases the vehicle; the customer who is driving the vehicle, who could be the owner; and then the insurance company who normally pays the invoice. All of them are my clients and I have to look after all of their different demands. I'm dealing with the man in the street right up to large corporations. Certain corporations can have the worst CSR values, although the person in the street sometimes conveniently forgets their values when its suits them. Some of my clients were better than others during the pandemic. Some continued to pay us on time, or earlier in some cases. Others were avoiding their responsibility and used the pandemic as an excuse.

When I talk about CSR-led clients, I talk about the bigger corporates who will have different values.

3. **What CSR advice would you give to someone who wants to start up a new business venture post this pandemic?**

Start with your purchase supply chain and the people you will be spending money with. Buy your goods and raw materials from people you like and trust, including people who you can have those difficult conversations with, if and when something like this pandemic happens again. Once you get support from your supply chain, the right type of customers will gravitate to you because it will show in your product and/or service — how you conduct your business.

I also think some businesses, with their business heads on, will be of the view that CSR is fluffy. It is not. It's about doing the best job you can for the best value that you can. It will come at a cost, because it is more expensive to operate ethically and to not cut corners. But this can transition to become normal business practice, where operating and providing services authentically and ethically won't be so expensive.

4. **How do you think a company can improve its engagement and support, with and from their employees, regarding the company's CSR core values?**

Respect with a capital 'R.' Respect your employees enough to keep them informed of the company's progress and growth. If you respect your employees and treat them as partners in the business, then those employees who appreciate your ethos and CSR values will go the extra mile for you and enhance your business and values. For some people it's only about the money, and you will never have loyalty from them.

Most people in my industry are very wary of good employers or employers looking after their interests. But once they start to realize that you're genuinely looking after them, they appreciate it and value it. They recognize a fair return for what they put in. Our industry is an ageing trade and we are not getting a younger generation coming through.

5. **What legacy would you like to leave behind as an entrepreneur?**

Trust. I would like employees, customers and suppliers to say I was trustworthy. Always spoke my mind, even if it was a message that was not going to be well received, but you always knew where you stood.

Chapter 7

CSR
AND THE
NEXT
GENERATION

THE NEW WORLD

The time will come when we'll re-emerge from the pandemic like butterflies that have been cocooned in a chrysalis, waiting for the new, safe dawn.

Things have changed, lives have changed, and they'll continue to change until the crisis has passed. Through the course of the global pandemic, we've learned that everything is connected. The virus has touched all of humanity, and as happens at moments of great change we will emerge with new clarity about our systems – political, economic, social and ecological. We're gaining new insight into what's strong, what's weak, what's corrupt, what matters and what doesn't.

While the pandemic has managed to push climate change out of the headlines, for now at least, the threat to the planet has not gone away. We now know we can expect to experience more shocks from extreme weather patterns and other types of pandemics.

We will all now want companies and organizations to operate with their hearts and minds, and we'll be looking to them to rethink their global value chains. Over the years, business responsibility has matured, shifting towards values – the values of customers, employees and investors. This shift will be accelerated by the global pandemic, as companies will need to pivot quickly towards values like inclusion, empathy and the environment. Responsibility, humanity and impact are now more entrenched than ever in the corporate sector. The pandemic has influenced our values, on a personal level and as brands and companies.

Consequently, sustainability will be seen as a bigger core brand value than any business could have imagined. This will come as climate change, plastic pollution and reducing waste continue to dominate global headlines. However, companies will need to ensure that none of their CSR initiatives are pure marketing tools, because they'll face a consumer and media backlash. Instead, CSR initiatives will become really integral to core brand values and be repositioned at the starting point of business strategies. They will then be 'sincerely' filtered through to all of an organization's internal and external communications, operations and delivery.

This means that creating a human connection between a brand and its audiences will be of paramount importance. The PR strategy will need to be driven by emotion and have a distinct human element, in order to be more meaningful and lead to a growing focus on expert, local and enthusiastic micro-influencers, instead of macro-influencers. Everything will be drilled down, as consumers endure constant information overload and will want to engage with businesses on their own terms.

The best campaigns will focus on creating not just customers, but true fans who are passionate about the brand. They'll produce dedicated cheerleaders who proactively search for information and become active advocates for the business. If we rewind to ten years ago, this is what social media marketing set out to do, but it somehow lost its way.

We know that money makes the world go 'round, and we know that investor interest in ESG – those cardinal environmental, social and governance factors – has already gone mainstream. Many experts believe this trend will continue to grow, with socially responsible investing gradually becoming the new normal.

Over the last ten years, there's been big interest in CSR from the financial sector, with over 90% of the largest banking and finance firms now filing sustainability reports. This is not new, but what is new is the interest in using the information for investment decisions. A study by Oxford University found that more than 80% of mainstream investors now consider ESG factors when making investment decisions.[34] The numbers are compelling: globally, there are now $22.89 trillion in assets being professionally managed under responsible investment strategies, an increase of 25% since 2014. For context, that total exceeds the GDP of the entire US economy!

This upswing in investor interest, along with consumer and employee demand, will bring CSR impact to the top of the agenda at boardroom and C-Suite meetings. As a result, embedding social impact into their business and brand strategies will no longer be a choice for companies. Rather, it will become a necessity if an organization wants to thrive and compete for talent, customers and investors. CSR will further creep into the boardroom as customers expect more from brands, and new investor funds crop up exclusively for companies with strong ESG performance.

Sustainable and inclusive growth will prove to be good for business, and companies that align their growth strategies with their ethics will be a step ahead in 'future-proofing' their business. Those that don't will be signing their own death warrant.

Escalating expectations from consumers, decreasing confidence in the public sector and a vacuum of leadership on environmental and social issues means that businesses must rethink how they deliver value to the consumer, rebalance scale and mass production against personalization, and practice what they preach when they address marketing issues and work ethics. Ignoring these imperatives can pose significant risks to a brand.

In the new world that emerges after the pandemic, consumers will be making new choices about how they travel, shop, work and conduct their daily lives. As they make their choices, corporate reputations will matter to a greater degree than ever. There will be long memories of how companies behaved and treated people during this crisis.

One of the things I think we need to see is a box that all new start-ups tick when they go through various registration and licensing processes, stating that CSR is at the heart of their brand values. Such a commitment would help ensure that CSR isn't just a marketing tool, but a fundamental criterion all businesses need to adhere to. Imagine if it were given the same weight as doing your taxes.

With such a statement of intent, your customers, your workforce and the media will all know that you've ticked the box and that you can't be operating without it. This has to be the future, and a truly global requirement.

PREDICTIONS

The challenges ahead are real, and companies will need to tap into human truths and acknowledge human potential. Here are just a few of the life-altering issues I foresee us all confronting in the years ahead.

1. Dealing with Future Disasters

From wildfires to extreme weather events, natural disasters are expected to increase. While emergency services and front-line responders will work hard to scale up their capacity to address the escalating risks, businesses must be prepared for the impact natural disasters will have on their operations, employees and the communities they serve. The ability to rapidly deploy assistance, and thoughtfully support stakeholders in the event of a crisis, will create immense opportunities for companies and become part of their CSR values and business plans.

2. **Joined-Up Thinking and More Global Collaboration**
Fighting the global pandemic in 2020 has shown that we're all connected, and going forward there will be demand for more companies to collaborate with their peers – including their competitors – to address future challenges COVID-19 has brought about. More of these alliances will be expected to help expand access to renewable energy, address plastic waste, innovate new packaging materials and promote sustainable agriculture.

3. **Diversity and Inclusiveness**
During the writing of this book, ethnic diversity is an issue that has galloped up the news agenda as we've witnessing global protests over racial inequality. Companies have realized that diversity and inclusion are more than just an add-on, but most still have a long way to go when it comes to achieving meaningful goals. Remember the backlash against Gucci's polo neck jumper that resembled blackface?[35] Or the outrage over H&M's advertising image of a black child in a 'monkey' hoodie?[36] There are many other examples of tone-deaf marketers, and a majority of stakeholders are fed up that change around diversity and equity is not happening faster.

At the same time, demographics are shifting and companies can no longer ignore the business case to build a diverse and inclusive workforce. For example, data from the Economic Policy Institute shows that by 2030, a majority of the US's young workers will be people of colour.[37] Employees will demand that their employers take action on diversity-related issues, as they will feel empowered and expect more from their bosses.

A *Harvard Business Review* study with the Technical University of Munich showed that start-ups with diverse teams generate higher revenue, make decisions faster and better, and are more innovative.[38] Investors will see diversity as an indicator of a company's long-term success, and its ability to attract the best talent and be more innovative and competitive. Inevitably, investors will use their influence to push harder for gender and racial/ethnic diversity.

4. The Future Is Generation Z

There has been a growing trend for companies to craft their CSR strategies around their employees' passions, as opposed to focusing mainly on their external brand reputation and PR. As we discussed earlier, today's employees – particularly millennials – expect to work for a company that 'gives back.' But, the key here is that they want to give back on their own terms, and have a say in what causes their company supports and how and when they volunteer their time. It's important for businesses to survey their workforce and forge relationships with non-profits in areas that their people are passionate about, and with charity partners that allow them to customize employee engagement opportunities. Leading companies are listening to and supporting the needs of their employees in these areas, and providing tools and resources to elevate their voices.

Also, we'll see the conversation shift from millennials to Gen Z, who were born between 1995 and 2010, and their influence and impact on the workplace culture and society. These ten- to 30-year-olds represent is a generation who are true digital natives: from childhood they've been exposed to the internet, social networks and powerful to mobile devices. Companies will need to gain an insight into this generation's views on climate change, diversity and the role a corporation should play in social and environmental issues. A McKinsey & Company study found four core Gen Z behaviours, all anchored in one element: this generation's search for truth.[39]

First, the study revealed that many from Gen Z value individual expression and avoid labels. Next, they may be inclined to mobilize themselves for a variety of causes, believing in the efficacy of dialogue to solve conflicts and improve the world. Meanwhile, they relate to institutions in an analytical and pragmatic way, which is why Gen Z has been called the 'True Gen.' And, it seems that many of them will be more idealistic, increasingly confrontational and less willing to accept diverse points of view. These behaviours will influence the way many Gen Zers view the concept of consumerism and their relationships with brands.

Companies will want to be attuned to three implications for this generation: consumption as access rather than possession; consumption as an expression of individual identity; consumption as a matter of ethical concern.

Coupled with technological advances, this generational shift is transforming the consumer landscape in a way that cuts across all socioeconomic brackets and extends beyond Gen Z, permeating the whole demographic pyramid.

5. Increased Employee Activism

Employees are reshaping corporate culture by calling for social and environmental change. And so, when a company isn't meeting its employees' needs on topics such as equal pay, climate action, diversity and inclusion, we can expect employees to find new ways to encourage action. For instance, they're likely to start social media conversations, writing frank and revealing blogs or op-ed commentary on how their employer is at fault.

This past year, both the annual Academy Awards (the Oscars) and the BAFTA awards were blasted for a lack of diversity in cinema. At the BAFTAs in London, we saw actors Joaquin Phoenix, Rebel Wilson and the organization's president, Prince William, criticize a dearth of diversity among the nominated creators and performers, saying the issue could no longer be ignored.

There have also been many employee-led initiatives within the technology industry, including large-scale walkouts at companies like Google, demanding action on sexual misconduct, a lack of diversity and other issues that have plagued the sector.

6. Technology and Artificial Intelligence

Technology innovation, in fields such as artificial intelligence (AI), are changing the world, touching all types of enterprises. AI itself is helping organizations forge trust with stakeholders. There's the notion of 'AI for Good,' as a means to reduce risks to businesses, employees and customers. It's making government more transparent and efficient, healthcare more effective and accessible, cities more liveable and the planet more sustainable. When harnessed and used effectively, this technology will be able to do things we've never even conceived of before.

According to data by PricewaterhouseCoopers, 72% of business leaders in the US believe AI will be the business advantage of the future.[40]

New, emerging technologies are influencing real-time data collection and reporting, and new methods of communication and number-crunching, transforming CSR. Companies spend a lot of time, effort and resources to prepare CSR reports, yet how many of these documents are read and are actually meaningful? Without integration of CSR into business processes, and without CSR reports bringing tangible value, this yearly activity becomes a drain on business resources. However, things are changing as technology makes it easier to enhance and focus on CSR, particularly by addressing the challenges of data reporting.

For example, companies and organizations can now produce and disseminate their own research and findings through different media channels utilizing virtual reality, videos and interactive. These data distribution tools reach a wider audience, because they're far more engaging and relatable, especially when compared to conventional data presentation formats, such as pie charts. Companies can use these channels to provide sustainability information in ways that are more interesting and enjoyable for readers. And this, in turn, could help businesses engage with new and different audiences.

A good example of this is from Heineken, the beer brand, which launched an interactive sustainability report, 'Brewing a Better World,' where the information was presented using GIFs.

Another great example is Chiquita. The global banana company does a lot of work behind the scenes to support its farming communities, through building and renovating school infrastructure and making key advances in farm management. By putting a QR code symbol on its well-known blue sticker, Chiquita allowed its customers to scan their banana and unlock 360 videos that transported them to the farms themselves. This allowed consumers to not only see the work that their purchase contributed to, but gave a platform directly to the people behind the product. Here, augmented reality (AR) let these people tell their own story in a far more compelling way than any press release, article or talking-head spokesman could.

At the same time, blockchain technology can help create more transparent, streamlined and accountable management systems for businesses, consumers and countries. Blockchain is a system of recording information that makes it difficult to alter or hack. It's effectively a digital ledger of transactions that is duplicated and distributed across the entire network of computer systems. It could help reduce emissions and waste, as well as address manufacturer and distribution problems across the supply chains.

It's playing a big role in allowing companies to log every transaction, which has been invaluable for businesses with a far-flung supply chain. The result: a more streamlined, cost-efficient and waste-reducing network, every step of the way.

The apparel giant Levi Strauss & Co. has already committed to rolling out blockchain technology in its factories, to increase efficiency. LVMH Moët Hennessy, the luxury goods company that owns powerhouse brands like Louis Vuitton, Dom Perignon, Givenchy, TAG Heuer and Christian Dior, has begun using blockchain to track authentic products and fight counterfeiting.

Blockchain has the potential to create new societal awareness and reward those who choose to act more sustainably. It can help build a framework that allows us to understand how our carbon emissions work, educating us on our personal effect on the planet. Therefore, blockchain should be playing a much more integral role in terms of changing the way whole countries, governments, industries and individuals are able to see the impact their behaviour is having on the environment.

7. Big Data Will Be Big News

Now, accessible, real-time CSR reporting has become the norm. Technologies such as blockchain, big data and AI allow organizations and consumers to understand and find the correlations between what would otherwise be complex, unintelligible statistics.

Data technology is helping the process of putting a price on impacts and externalities. This pushes through the creation of methodologies to accurately assess and evaluate how upside consequences can be monetized. The growth of big data analytics allows 'big picture' sustainability reporting, providing useful tools to measure and analyze traditionally intangible ESG indicators in a more coherent and integrated way.

Big data has also been used in human development. The UN established Global Pulse, a big data lab in New York, with satellite offices in Kampala and Jakarta. In Indonesia, Global Pulse applied mobile phone data to understand food price fluctuations, and in Uganda it was used to chart population movements.

Meanwhile, the donation of data by companies, also known as 'data philanthropy,' has become a CSR activity in and of itself. IBM and other businesses host 'Open Data' events ('jams' and 'hackathons') in which governments, NGOs and companies are encouraged to release data that can be used for constructive social or environmental purposes.

8. Business Innovation

Innovation is imperative for long-term survival, and it goes beyond new product development. It means radically re-evaluating areas of your business, such as strategy, business processes, operations and management models. Consultant and author Peter Drucker, whose writings contributed to the philosophical and practical foundations of the modern corporation, said that "every single social and global issue of our day is a business opportunity in disguise."[41] There are numerous examples of highly successful startups, now global companies, that have done just that!

CORPORATE SOCIAL RESPONSIBILITY IS NOT PUBLIC RELATIONS

The Nutriplanet programme of food products company Danone analyzed nutritional, socioeconomic and cultural data on the habits and health issues of populations in 52 countries for purposeful product development. After studying the diets of Brazil's youth, for example, Danone reformulated a best-selling cheese by reducing sugar and adding vitamins. In Bangladesh, children eat 600,000 servings a week of Danone's Shok ti-Doi, a market-targeted, nutrient-rich yogurt. R&D also extends into packaging, where in Senegal the company developed a carton composed of local grain and a little milk that can be stored at room temperature.

Vodafone, the telecom company, obtained a grant from the British government's Department for International Development to cover initial R&D for a new service that would give people in less developed countries access to financial services. The venture, M-Pesa, was kept separate from other Vodafone businesses. Today M-Pesa is managed by the company's national subsidiaries and is one of its most important offerings, accounting for 18% of the revenue of Kenyan subsidiary Safaricom. The experience encouraged Vodafone to link up with philanthropies and government agencies to experiment in other areas, such as agricultural information services and applications to remotely monitor and manage home energy consumption.

9. Community Engagement

Long-term partnerships and relationships are going to become increasingly important for businesses, which will need to invest more in local community ties.

Businesses can help tackle community problems, as organizations and institutions dealing with them don't have enough resources to finance the necessary change. The current model in place to deal with social issues, which includes NGOs and philanthropies, is well meaning but often scales with difficulty. Issues such as healthcare, access to water or education and climate change would be much better addressed with a deeper collaboration between businesses, NGOs and governments.

As part of this metamorphosis, we'll see companies move towards the idea of 'belonging,' to create an environment where everyone can thrive and feel engaged. Belonging will be a competitive advantage.

10. Continued Rise of Plant-Based Diets

In 2019 we saw the rise of plant-based diets driven by consumer interest in vegan and flexitarian diets. Beyond the obvious health benefits, this was driven by growing awareness of the environmental impact of meat production and concerns over animal welfare. The trend has been accelerated by social media, giving rise to a more pervasive plant-based lifestyle. Celebrities like Ariana Grande, Miley Cyrus, Alicia Silverstone and Sia are some of the well-known figures who don't eat animal products, while #vegan has more than 87 million posts on Instagram. Veganism is a hot topic; the number of Google searches on the subject has spiked worldwide in recent years.

The UK market for meat-free foods was reportedly worth £740 million in 2018, according to market researchers Mintel, up from £539 million only three years ago. Companies are staying on trend, and UK supermarket chains have been stocking more vegan options, including the fast-growing beyond meat brand's burgers and sausages, to keep up with consumers' evolving food preferences. A range of fast-food companies – from the bakery Greggs to giants like McDonald's, Burger King and KFC – have launched, or announced plans for, vegan options in the UK.

11. Kindness

For years, kindness in business has been regarded as a weakness and not a strength. Now, though, consumers increasingly look for their personal values to be represented when they spend their money. This expectation is growing, particularly as personal sensitivities have been inflamed by the pandemic and the BLM movement. Today, kindness is regarded as a business asset, and as we step further into the future, authentic kindness will be seen as a business necessity. This will be especially true as we see organizations judged on their actual behaviour, rather than their claimed attributes. Those who pass the test will enjoy substantial consumer and employee loyalty. Those who fail will be called out and face negative publicity.

The future is promising, as changing attitudes in business and society foster a new way of doing things. Increasingly, word of mouth is the way business is won, and how you increase your audience and referrals. Kindness and generosity are instrumental to this approach. There's also a growing global appetite for a kinder, gentler society, where staff are given more time off to spend with family and friends and companies care about the environment. Therefore, to create strategic, long-lasting positive change in and from your business, brands will need to cultivate genuine kindness and put it at the heart of their strategy. This will endure, and strengthen the value of your business.

Kindness will be the kind of business asset that will not depreciate over time.

IN CONVERSATION... WITH JESSICA ATKINS

In the summer of 2019, while shopping, I serendipitously met Jessica Atkins, part of a new generation of entrepreneurs who are shaking things up. Jessica is behind the sustainable fashion label waYst, an I have no doubt that this small operation will soon be transforming the world of business. Jessica is already giving us consumers better choices. This is both a business and an entrepreneur to watch out for!

I managed to interview Jessica in May 2020, while she was busy making gowns for the UK's front-line health workers.

1. **What inspired you to set up waYst clothing? Why do you want to do business differently?**

I graduated with a costume construction degree from the Royal Central School of Speech and Drama in 2019. Before studying, I never considered the stages required to make a single garment of clothing, but this led me to question, "How were clothes sold so cheaply?" I became conscious of the materials used in mass production, the dyeing processes and the less glamorous side of fashion.

I began to investigate the ethical and sustainable aspects of the clothing industry and was disheartened by the truths surrounding fast fashion, from the excessive waste in landfill sites, and the devastating carbon impact of manufacturers, to the tragic lives of exploited people working in unsafe environments where they receive meagre salaries and no worker's rights. I was also saddened by feelings that I had contributed to these injustices, which changed the way I purchased clothing and made my choices.

For my final degree show, I created a tutu and chose to use dyes that I naturally sourced from vegetables, including onion skins and avocado stones. While researching synthetic dyes I learned about their toxic effects on the environment and humans. This led me to investigate alternative techniques for dyeing, and I began to experiment with flowers, nettles, beetroot and cabbage, which produced beautiful shades of natural colour.

All this led to me to setting up waYst, inspired by my vision to create a clothing and accessory brand that is ethical and sustainable. Its ethos engages with many concerns around fast fashion consumerism and builds honest and transparent relationships through its brand identity and consumer loyalty. waYst is in its first year, and it has a social conscience and a twist. This twist derives from the concept that waste has negative connotations and is viewed as a by-product, which is discarded and useless. waYst challenges this concept by using waste products in a new and innovative way to produce beautiful, naturally-dyed products.

2. What does a sustainable business mean to you?

As a sustainable business, waYst creates, delivers and promotes ethical value to all its 'waYsters' and contributes towards a respectful and greener future for the planet and its inhabitants. Each piece is a one-off and is delivered with a handcrafted, naturally-dyed 'thank you' card. waYst creates each piece with love and passion, and as the company is in its early stages of development, everything is being designed and handmade from my home.

Every step of the process has been given careful consideration, including the choice to use hemp instead of cotton. Growing hemp is generally an eco-friendly and sustainable process, as it does not require as much water for growing crops such as cotton. It uses far less pesticides, is renewable and benefits the soil by separating carbon dioxide from the atmosphere.

3. Who are you customers and followers? What do you think they're looking for?

The waYst customers and followers are known as waYsters, and are a varied audience who belong to the waYst tribe. They all share the waYst vision, which supports their values for an environmentally friendly planet, offers excellent quality, durability of products and love of the unique, one-off creations of artisan craftwork. Our customers care about the journey behind the products, support the authenticity of the brand and share in the development of new, innovative products.

4. **What do you want to see established businesses do more of?**

Create an inclusive environment where employees are paid fairly, enjoy coming to work and take pride in the growth of the company. I'd like to see established businesses support developing ones like waYst.

5. **Do you think there's a future for businesses without any CSR values?**

I hope not. I think that our culture has become more socially aware in so many ways, where people now care about what they eat, how things are made, plastic bags, etc. There is an overwhelming shared consciousness between my friends who really care about a sustainable culture that's engaging, transparent and ethically responsible. In their own ways, they're all supporting green issues and are advocates for social justice, and the waYst branding really supports all this.

6. **What changes do you want to effect in business and in the fashion world?**

The promotion of small, ethical businesses where fashion is sustainable and affordable. I would like to see more equality within society, where people and their work are justifiably valued and where quirky, high-quality, traditional and artisan craftwork is promoted over mass production.

7. **What could policymakers be better at to support conscious businesses like yours, whether that's local or global?**

I would love to see policymakers invest in affordable studio spaces and small shops, for start-up businesses like waYst who want to introduce new concepts to new audiences. I think this is positive for both policymakers and innovators.

8. Do you think there is a shift in thinking, particularly since the global pandemic, that globalization no longer works?

Definitely – the virus outbreak has been a human tragedy and a global economic disaster. At the height of the pandemic, I was happy to see Britain's textile industry making a comeback, by helping to make masks and PPE (personal protective equipment). This is now being produced in the UK, and I hope this kind of support continues, and becomes a permanent feature, following the pandemic.

Social media was a wonderful platform to share the skills and efforts of British people wanting to support the NHS, and voluntarily offer their hearts and time to make PPE locally, during the height of the pandemic in the UK.

My mum is an NHS midwife and I created a hemp, naturally-dyed mask for her, which at the time really caught on and led to big orders for face masks, which waYst was naturally dying from nettles, vegetable waste and flowers on 100% natural hemp. I'm proud to have made an alternative mask that's safe to use. Skin is the largest organ of the body, and breathing in noxious synthetic dyes from close-fitting masks is concerning and potentially health threatening.

9. **Has COVID-19 affected your business? What are you doing differently?**

Dyeing workshops for children that I had set up for Easter 2020 had to be cancelled. Also, as a new company, I had made plans to collect waste products from local cafes and markets to dye my fabrics, which I now could not do. Instead, I had to find new ways of doing things, and started to use waste products from home, and I also went to the forest.

Plus, an unexpected order for the creation of naturally-dyed hemp masks at that time really changed things, which have since become a popular accessory. I would never have dreamt of making these when I set up my business.

IN CONVERSATION...
WITH DAVID KATZ

It's not every day that you get to speak to a real visionary, but I did in May 2020. David Katz, the founder and CEO of Plastic Bank, is a true change-maker. Plastic Bank empowers the regenerative society, helping the world stop the proliferation of ocean plastic while improving the lives of collector communities.

Plastic Bank is an internationally recognized root-cause solution to the ocean plastic crisis. It builds ethical recycling ecosystems in coastal communities, and reprocesses the materials for reintroduction into the global supply chain as 'Social Plastic.'

David is a steward of the earth and a champion of social impact, whose humanitarian work has earned him international recognition. He was recipient of the 2017

UN Lighthouse Award for Planetary Health, the Paris Climate Conference's 2015 Sustainia Community Award, and was named Entrepreneur's Organization's 2014 Global Citizen of the Year. And then there's my favourite: being named one of the world's most compassionate entrepreneurs by *Salt Magazine*. David has been featured in *Forbes*, *TIME*, *Fast Company* and *National Geographic*.

Our thought-provoking conversation stayed with me long afterwards.

1. **Has it been easy for you to convince corporates to collaborate with you to prevent the flow of plastic into our oceans?**

Has it been easy? No. You're meeting people with resistance because no one wants to be wrong and everyone wants to be right. But, when you're talking to the right person, with the right language and the right paradigm, then certainly it's not as hard convincing someone against their will. Speaking to someone in a supply chain, saying that they have to spend more money on material, is not an easy conversation, and you can also find that the NGO shows up with all the 'buts.'

We encourage corporates to behave better and teach the not-for-profits how to work with corporates. In fact, the not-for-profits need to become 'for profit' themselves and change their operations and thinking. The people that these charities want to help around the world are on their backs and they need to be on their feet. Yet, what you find is that while these charities do take vulnerable people from their back to their knees, these people's hands are still out begging, never really fixing the root cause.

And that's because these charities themselves are on their knees, with their hands out, also begging. For-profit businesses are already on their feet, and that's when you can truly lift someone from their back and put them on their feet.

Core values are important because they come from deep within us. And when we take the time to discover our core values – who we are, what's really important, and what we stand for – they guide every action and business decision that we make. At Plastic Bank, 'becoming' is a core value and is a continuous, never-ending journey. The origin of the idea of Plastic Bank came to me in three thoughts. It wasn't born out of the idea of monetizing waste; the second thought was dealing with all the corporates. But it was the third thought where Plastic Bank was born, and I owe everything to this third thought, which was to slowly become the person who can create change. And when we shift our attention to who we need to be, then the doing becomes easy. Thinking is being human. This is life at its essence.

You can't teach people or convince people to recycle. But at Plastic Bank we can provide something that is better for people, and that's when it becomes powerful enough for people to listen and adopt it over time. Learning about who you need to speak to was not easy, because you spend a lot of time in the wrong places. But, once you learn, and have taken all the lessons to get to the right place, then speaking to the right people is not as hard. The difficulty was in the learning.

2. **What have been the challenges to Plastic Bank operating in the developing nations you're working in?**

Challenges will occur all the time. We've had people murdered, shot, and faced all kinds of things. But this hasn't stopped us, and challenges are not insurmountable. Your power comes through when you face challenges and recognize that the obstacles on your path are part of your journey. Challenges make you creative and are a gift. A great book to explain this is *The Obstacle is the Way* by Ryan Holiday.

Everyone has a favourite radio station, which is 'radio station WFM' – *what's in it for me?* So, we at Plastic Bank tell them 'what's in it for you' is that you can put your child through school, earn money, have access to medicines, you can buy cooking fuel.

We've been creative to find solutions and come up with a very comprehensive programme for the ideological and for our faith-based collectors. It is called *Social Plastic Faith Movement*, and encourages the parishioners to bring their recycling as offerings for the collection. When I was at the Vatican I heard about the nuns who invite themselves to eat at the houses of the poor, where the vulnerable feel empowered that they have something to give. There's something very empowering for the vulnerable, when they feel that they have something to give.

3. **Do you believe that corporates are genuine with their CSR values, or are some just paying lip service?**

No, no, no. Nope, nope! They are a bunch of bullshit. When it comes to shareholders, it's the devil incarnate. Publicly-traded companies is where the shareholders win at the expense of all other things. The structure itself is wrong – it's where people make investments in the company for things that may occur in the future, for the results they want in the future, and people can go to jail if they don't create this thing that doesn't actually exist, and doesn't deliver on the expectations. The entire company revolves around this quarterly reporting, which is about taking and taking to give to the few shareholders, and about extracting revenue from society.

All I see is companies degrading society, polluting the planet, creating catastrophes and trying to sequester their taxation from the population. How dare businesses think they've gotten where they are without the roads, the police, the hospitals, and the schools and everything else. How dare they think that they've received that profitability without society and the taxation. They don't want to pay their share of taxes.

They all have beautiful mottos, but it's all bullshit. CSR is corporate bullshit, which is corporate storytelling. CSR is all about screaming so loudly that I can't hear what you say, because what you do screams so loudly. There's this quote: "We have the opportunity to choose who our children's parents will be. Some choose that their children's parents will steward the earth, or that my children's parents will be compassionate, loving, giving, generous."

What is actually better than CSR is authenticity in the way you show up on the planet. CSR is such an oxymoron. Why do you need to communicate it? Just show up and do well for the planet, do well for your staff, do well for everybody. Just show up and do right. It's not about doing better – do right and be human.

By doing right, you won't have to tell anyone. When you do that, of course, people will want to work for you, buy from you, support you and say good things about you. And that's because it's authentic and real.

4. Can you lead with CSR values and still be profitable?
Yes. We're a multi-billion-dollar organization, where we have a hundred-million-dollar valuation. We have just begun and we're not even trying! The more abundance you create in the world, the more it comes back. Companies have been operating for profit first, and then for purpose and people. Now, people are seeing through this and waking up. So, yes, of course you can be profitable. Being authentic is the root of profitability, and when you are doing that everyone is rooting for you.

Plastic Bank only wins as a brand when the collector powerfully wins. When our collector members' lives change, then we get to win and participate in that change. When we win, they win, and they recognize that. Even our recyclers on the ground win when our collectors win. A consumer wins when we all win. The brand will only win when the consumer wins; the consumer will only win when the collector wins.

5. Regarding your 'Social Plastic Collection Credits' initiative, using a blockchain system, do you think this type of technology will become widespread in the future for corporates, when implementing their CSR goals?

Authenticity has to spread everywhere, and blockchain develops authenticity. To have something that you can rely on truthfully is enough for business. Blockchain also frees up time and is a digital platform that empowers people to become automated ATMs, and it's revolutionizing recycling plastic at the same time. At Plastic Bank our ambition is for everything to be automated.

6. What do you think the global financial impact of the COVID-19 pandemic will be on vulnerable communities? Has it accelerated your plans to expand Plastic Bank in other regions?

It has been devastating and has plunged people into poverty. We can only continue what we're doing at Plastic Bank, where we created advances for our collectors, who can borrow from us instead of going to loan sharks.

I think people will understand that this self-autonomy is an opportunity to find additional income, which they will need more than ever.

7. Do you think it should become law globally that every company has a credible CSR policy?

Should it be law that they don't degrade the earth? Yes! If you inflict pain on societies and on the Earth, then you should not be able to operate.

8. **What legacy do you want to leave behind?**
I think Plastic Bank is multi-generational, and I'm planting the seeds of a tree that will blossom with my passing.

Conclusion

THE FOURTH REVOLUTION

Consumer loyalty can be fickle, as there is ever more choice. For a business, that means that if you aren't 'walking the walk and talking the talk,' your consumers will go elsewhere.

Brands need to be able to stand out in a crowded marketplace, and they can do this by standing for values that are authentic to you. The year 2020 accelerated the conversation about CSR and how brands act. We've arrived at a place where consumers, employees and investors are now putting increasing pressure on businesses to make meaningful contributions to the greater social good.

As we step further into the 'Fourth Revolution' – a term coined by the World Economic Forum – we're part of an exciting new era that builds on the previous one. The First Revolution was the industrial revolution; the second was about electricity; the third was digital and the age of the internet. In the Fourth Revolution we all have the will to do better, and be better. We recognize that, as brands and organizations, we can no longer plunder the planet or profit off the backs of the impoverished and vulnerable. We have the technology to behave better.

In building on the Third Revolution, this fourth wave is characterizsed by new technologies such as AI and autonomous vehicles, which are merging with humans' physical lives. This has the potential to raise global income levels and improve the quality of life for populations around the world.

The insights from the thought leaders I interviewed for this book are coming to pass, like eerie prophecies. I can't shake off Mark Holden's warning in Chapter One, where he spoke about the debt this global pandemic would cause, which he believed wasn't being thought through by governments. We now know that the world is going through its biggest recession yet – one that some have warned will be more monumental than the one that followed the Second World War.

I've also been thinking about Vince Scudder describing us as having a goldfish's memory, saying we'd quickly forget about doing better for the planet once we emerged from lockdown. It seems Vince was right, as there's now a new kind of pollution to deal with: discarded facemasks, latex gloves and empty hand sanitizer bottles. In the UK, we've seen vast new amounts of litter being left on beaches, in parks and along nature trails, as people are socializing differently than before the lockdown – they're mainly congregating outdoors. And with that, a rash of careless behaviour has spawned mountains of litter.

CHANGING MEDIA LANDSCAPE

Every industry has been affected by the COVID-19 pandemic and communications is no exception. We're now navigating a completely different media landscape, driven by the shifts in information consumption patterns and cuts in advertising spend.

People globally are now spending more time with social and online content, and consumers have changed their consumption preferences, supporting brands that demonstrate purposeful messaging. Radio and TV audiences have grown, and in some markets print is actually witnessing a revival, with people reading newspapers – both digitally and in old-school hardcopy format – more frequently.

This shift demonstrates a real demand for credible information, in an age where purpose is the new communications currency. This means that communications teams have had to adapt to the shift, and they're working hard to help channels fulfil this increasing need for honest and relevant content. Websites of credible, trustworthy organizations, such as WHO and official government sites, are becoming increasingly important resources.

Consequently, communications professionals have had to change their own behaviours to rise to this challenge.

BEING CANCELLED

However, I do believe there are now more of us in business and in communities who want a different approach to the planet. We want 'better.'

We can see this in the conversations around diversity and inclusiveness, which grew in the weeks after the murder of George Floyd by four Minneapolis policemen was filmed and broadcast via social media around the world. It's continued to be part of wider business conversations and media debates. The issue of race is an integral component of CSR, and we've seen some of the best-known brands using their marketing channels to support these conversations. Netflix stated in May 2020, on Twitter: "To be silent is to be complicit. Black lives matter. We have a platform, and we have a duty to our Black members, employees, creators and talent to speak up."[42] Apple Music joined the 'Black Out Tuesday' campaign that took place on 2 June 2020 to support the movement, and Nike adapted its slogan with, "For once, Don't Do It."

Companies taking a stand on social issues has been a new phenomenon, rarely seen prior to last year. I believe this signals a new kind of thought leadership and PR, which isn't spin, or political correctness, or about being 'woke.'

Instead, it is about companies being assertive and making hard-headed business decisions for each message, weighing the costs and benefits to the bottom line. A great example of this was the skincare and beauty products brand Glossier, which announced on social media that it was delaying the launch of its latest product in an effort to focus attention, and its audience, on "the ongoing fight against racial injustice." The company also set aside $500,000 in the form of grants that will be distributed to Black-owned beauty businesses.[43]

We're now living in what is known as a 'cancel culture,' where people publicly withdraw their support for a company or an individual, and sometimes actively boycott them. This is a culture that thrives on social media, with conflicts quickly going viral. Barely a day goes by where someone isn't 'cancelled,' and in some cases cancel culture has turned into trolling online, with people facing horrendous abuse and even death threats. This has created a debate about an intolerant climate for free speech. And, it's created another tricky challenge for brands to navigate. The best of them will continue to be proactive about taking stands, in support of their fervently held values, as they did on diversity and inclusion.

While it's clear that consumers want brands to stand for something, 'woke washing' can be more damaging than doing nothing at all. There are two clear, practical reasons your business should stand for something. First, it's essential if consumers demand it, wanting your company to help them make a difference. Second, it's important if your employees and potential future talent are adamant about an issue.

This is not just a business trend; it's human nature! We like to align ourselves with causes that make us feel good. When brands nail 'social purpose,' it shows customers that the brand is something they can be proud to be associated with.

ESG

I've heard some thought leaders say that CSR is not the purpose of a business. On the contrary, I'd argue that it is. Every organization has a duty to be doing better for the planet, and you can't do that if CSR is not part of your purpose and strategy. Your CSR values have to be at the heart of your brand. They will then filter effortlessly into your collaborations, supply chains, operations and how you treat your staff. Do you think that if the fast-fashion retailer Boohoo had put its CSR values authentically at the heart of its business purpose it would have faced negative publicity for the worker exploitation scandal mentioned earlier? The narrative would have been different – it could have been a positive, reputation-polishing story for the business.

When your CSR values are your purpose, there's no room for error... and errors come at a cost, particularly with shareholders.

As this book has described, 2020 was a major turning point for ESG investing. There is now an unprecedented emphasis on knowing how corporations treated their stakeholders, in particular their employees and their customers, during the pandemic. Indeed, COVID-19 has altered society's values. Investors want to know a company's environmental, social and governance ratings alongside traditional financial metrics. This emphasis on ESG reflects a fundamental shift in investing, and it will continue to increase.

Investors are demanding greater corporate transparency and stakeholder accountability. For instance, they're ramping up pressure on banks, due to the increasing understanding of ESG factors like climate change, which are risks that must be managed. Investors want to ensure that they can continue to earn a return on their investment. Banks are feeling the pressure from their customers and from the public, as both want to engage with an institution that reflects their views and beliefs.

FINAL THOUGHTS

This is a time of increased urgency on these pressing issues. It calls for real, authentic collaboration for systemic change.

In this deeply political, polarized world, businesses have an even bigger role to play. They have a responsibility to help address the needs of people in areas where governments are failing. The questions for the global business community to address are now bigger than ever. Business leaders need to raise their voice to ensure that our open societies are preserved, and respected for inclusion and diversity. I hope that all businesses will rise to the occasion. We need companies to be assertive, and call out when things are wrong. They can't be overly cautious, and must take risks to bring about the changes our planet so desperately needs.

At the same time, we all need to be advocating for the reform of businesses around the world. This must be the responsibility of us all – the people – through the governments we elect, using our votes to ensure that we're living in a better, more just and sustainable world. We need better choices.

There are two quotes that I want to leave you with. The first is from the acclaimed author Nigel Watts, who originally wrote this for his Ph.D dissertation in Creative and Critical Writing, at the University of East Anglia. It has since been included in the foreword of his book, *Twenty Twenty*, which was republished in 2020 by his wife, Sahera

Chohan. The book, first published in 1995, predicted the global pandemic that took place this year.

"I believe the consequences are clear enough: consider yourself a bag of bones separate from your environment, and you will have the moral immunity to treat the world and its contents as things," Watts wrote. "Taken to its extreme, we have alienation and its concomitant fallout: crime, neurosis, the trashing of the environment. However, 'see' yourself as a leaf from a tree, quasi-autonomous perhaps, but essentially connected, and (so I wanted to propose) natural harmony will result."[44]

And then, there's this from the interview with Plastic Bank's David Katz featured in the previous chapter: "Just show up and do well for the planet, do well for your staff, do well for everybody. Just show up and do right. It's not about doing better – do right and be human."

Businesses now need to put CSR at the heart of their brands. Unfortunately, I've seen so many who have instead put PR at the heart of their companies. As a result, they lose their way and never do good by the planet. I want to help all types of corporates see the alternative, and to do right by their employees and customers. Businesses have a duty to do better, because we the consumer need better choices.

The communications industry has suffered for years with a bad reputation for spin and not enough inclusiveness. But when PR taps its real essence – the very human power of authentic storytelling – that's when the flow happens. And then, organizations don't have to worry about negative publicity, because they've put their CSR initiatives at the core of their business strategy.

That's when enduring success happens.

211

References

1. "RSA and Food Foundation survey shows changes in citizen attitudes to the food system," The Food Foundation, April 2020, https://foodfoundation.org.uk/covid_19/rsa-and-food-foundation-survey-shows-changes-in-citizen-attitudes-to-the-food-system/.

2. Barack Obama, "Remarks by the President in State of the Union Address," January 20, 2015, https://obamawhitehouse.archives.gov/the-press-office/2015/01/20/remarks-president-state-union-address-january-20-2015.

3. Mari Kooskora, Miia Juottonen and Katlin Cundiff, "The Relationship Between Corporate Social Responsibility and Financial Performance (A Case Study from Finland): How Businesses and Organizations Can Operate in a Sustainable and Socially Responsible Way," ResearchGate, January 2019, https://www.researchgate.net/publication/330373231_The_Relationship_Between_Corporate_Social_Responsibility_and_Financial_Performance_A_Case_Study_from_Finland_How_Businesses_and_Organizations_Can_Operate_in_a_Sustainable_and_Socially_Responsible_Way.

4. Rim Makni, Claude Francoeur and François Bellavance, "Causality Between Corporate Social Performance and Financial Performance: Evidence from Canadian Firms," *J Bus Ethics* 89, 409 (2009). https://cirano.qc.ca/actualite/2010-11-12/Makni_Francoeur_Bellavance%202009_Causality_CSP-FP.pdf.

5. Chih-Wei Peng and Mei-Ling Yang, "The Effect of Corporate Social Performance on Financial Performance: The Moderating Effect of Ownership Concentration," Journal of Business Ethics, Vol. 123, No. 1 (2014), 171–182, https://philpapers.org/rec/PENTEO-3.

6. Oscar Williams-Grut, "BlackRock vows to address climate change: 'Climate risk is investment risk'," yahoo!finance, January 14 2020, https://sg.news.yahoo.com/blackrock-climate-change-larry-fink-letter-sustainability-111946625.html.

7. Annachiara Biondi, "Prada is first in industry to sign sustainability-linked loan," Vogue Business, November 5 2019, https://www.voguebusiness.com/sustainability/prada-launches-sustainability-linked-loan.

8. Mark Evans, "8 out of 10 millennials prioritise responsible investing," The Better Society Network, last accessed November 26 2020, https://bettersociety.net/devere-millennials-ESG-finance.php.

9. Christopher Copper-Ind, "ESG investing is now mainstream, says deVere chief," International Investment, last accessed November 26 2020, https://www.internationalinvestment.net/news/4014491/esg-investing-mainstream-devere-chief.

10. Anita Roddick, *Business As Unusual: The Journey of Anita*, Thorsons, 2000.

11. "2015 Cone Communications/Ebiquity Global CSR Study," Cone, last accessed November 26 2020, https://www.conecomm.com/research-blog/2015-cone-communications-ebiquity-global-csr-study.

12. Magda B.L. Donia, Carol-Ann Tetrault Sirsly and Sigalit Ronen, "Employee Attributions of Corporate Social Responsibility as Substantive or Symbolic: Validation of a Measure," *Applied Psychology: An International Review*, Vol.66, No.1 (2017), https://iaap-journals.onlinelibrary.wiley.com/doi/abs/10.1111/apps.12081.

13. "Selfridges says goodbye to palm oil in own label range," Selfridges, May 6 2019, https://www.selfridges.com/GB/en/features/events/selfridges-selection-palm-oil-free/.

14. Edward Enninful, "Edward Enninful On Creating A Magazine Under Lockdown," Vogue, June 2 2020, https://www.vogue.co.uk/fashion/article/edward-enninful-magazine-lockdown.

15. Fred Dews, "Brookings Data Now: 75 Percent of 2025 Workforce Will Be Millennials," Brookings, last accessed November 26 2020, https://www.brookings.edu/blog/brookings-now/2014/07/17/brookings-data-now-75-percent-of-2025-workforce-will-be-millennials/.

16. "New Data on COVID-19 and Consumer Behavior," Astound Insights, March 16 2020, https://astoundcommerce.com/2020/03/16/new-data-on-covid-19-and-consumer-behavior/.

17. Lara Koslow and Jean Lee, "COVID-19 Consumer Sentiment Snapshot #1: Setting the Baseline," BCG, March 17 2020, https://www.bcg.com/publications/2020/covid-consumer-sentiment-survey-snapshot-3-30-20.

18. Dezan Shira & Associates, "Corporate Social Responsibility in India," India Briefing, March 23 2020, https://www.india-briefing.com/news/corporate-social-responsibility-india-5511.html/.

19. "2020 Theme: 'Yoga for Health – Yoga at Home'," United Nations, June 2020, https://www.un.org/en/observances/yoga-day.

20. Steve Hemsley, "Why brand storytelling should be the foundation of a growth strategy," Marketing Week, February 28 2016, https://www.marketingweek.com/why-brand-storytelling-should-be-the-foundation-of-a-growth-strategy/.

21. SustainAbility, "New Report Spotlights Media's Role in Corporate Social Responsibility And Sustainable Development Debate," CSR Wire, last accessed November 26 2020, https://www.csrwire.com/press_releases/16931-new-report-spotlights-media-s-role-in-corporate-social-responsibility-and-sustainable-development-debate.

22. Martha Henriques, "What is Future Planet?" BBC Future, February 3 2020, https://www.bbc.com/future/article/20200131-what-is-future-planet.

23. "Bloomberg Green," Bloomberg, https://www.bloomberg.com/green.

24. "The climate issue," *The Economist*, September 19 2019, https://www.economist.com/leaders/2019/09/19/the-climate-issue.

25. Marcela Kunova, "The Economist turns up the heat on climate change reporting," journalism.co.uk, September 19 2019, https://www.journalism.co.uk/news/the-economist-turns-up-the-heat-on-climate-change-reporting/s2/a744772/.

26. Digital News Report, "Overview," Last accessed November 15 2020, https://www.digitalnewsreport.org/survey/2020/overview-key-findings-2020/.

27. Mark Rice-Oxley, "In the ground and off the page: why we're banning ads from fossil fuels extractors," *The Guardian*, February 1 2020, https://www.theguardian.com/membership/2020/feb/01/ads-fossil-fuels-extractors-guardian-ban.

28. Russell Hotten, "Volkswagen: The Scandal explained," *BBC News*, December 10 2015, https://www.bbc.co.uk/news/business-34324772.

29. Oxfam Australia, "What She Makes," Last accessed November 15 2020, https://whatshemakes.oxfam.org.au/.

30. Molly Fleming, "Dove: We will make mistakes but we aren't going to lose the diversity game," Marketing Week, August 2 2018, https://www.marketingweek.com/dove-real-women-strategy/.

31. "Coldplay to pause touring until concerts are 'environmentally beneficial'," *BBC News*, November 21 2019, https://www.bbc.co.uk/news/entertainment-arts-50490700.

32. Julie Satow, "Leonardo DiCaprio Builds an Eco-Resort," *The New York Times*, April 3 2015, https://www.nytimes.com/2015/04/05/realestate/an-idea-hits-the-beach.html.

33. Edelman, "Edelman Trust Barometer Special Report on COVID 19 Demonstrates Essential Role of the Private Sector," Last accessed November 15 2020, https://www.edelman.com/research/covid-19-brand-trust-report.

34. "'Better data needed' on measures of sustainability in business," University of Oxford, April 6 2017, https://www.ox.ac.uk/news/2017-04-06-better-data-needed-measures-sustainability-business

35. Morwenna Ferrier, "Gucci withdraws $890 jumper after blackface backlash," *The Guardian*, February 7 2019, https://www.theguardian.com/fashion/2019/feb/07/gucci-withdraws-jumper-blackface-balaclava.

36. "H&M apologises over 'racist' image of black boy in hoodie," *BBC Newsbeat*, January 8 2018, http://www.bbc.co.uk/newsbeat/article/42603960/hm-apologises-over-racist-image-of-black-boy-in-hoodie.

37. Valerie Wilson, "People of color will be a majority of the American working class in 2032," Economic Policy Institute, June 9 2016, https://www.epi.org/publication/the-changing-demographics-of-americas-working-class/.

38. Rocio Lorenzo and Martin Reeves, "How and Where Diversity Drives Financial Performance," *Harvard Business Review*, January 30 2018, https://hbr.org/2018/01/how-and-where-diversity-drives-financial-performance.

39. Tracy Francis and Fernanda Hoefel, "'True Gen': Generation Z and its implications for companies," McKinsey & Company, November 12 2018, https://www.mckinsey.com/industries/consumer-packaged-goods/our-insights/true-gen-generation-z-and-its-implications-for-companies.

40. "Bot.me: How artificial intelligence is pushing man and machine closer together," PWC, April 2017, https://www.pwc.com/CISAI?WT.mc_id=CT1-PL52-DM2-TR1-LS4-ND6-BPA1-CN_CIS-AI-AIsocial.

41. "Opportunity in Disguise," Drucker Institute, January 14 2011, https://www.drucker.institute/news-post/opportunity-in-disguise/.

42. Netflix, Twitter post, May 30 2020, https://twitter.com/netflix/status/1266829242353893376?lang=en.

43. "Grant Initiative for Black-Owned Beauty Businesses," Glossier, June 11 2020, https://www.glossier.com/blog/grants.

44. Nigel Watts, *Twenty Twenty*, Self-published, August 2020, https://www.amazon.co.uk/Twenty-Nigel-Watts/dp/B08F6YCZTV.